Banishing Fear
from Your Life

Banishing Fear from Your Life

CHARLES D. BASS

DOUBLEDAY & COMPANY, INC.
GARDEN CITY, NEW YORK
1986

Dedicated to

My Mother
Doris L. Bass
An Excellent Model for
Faith Thinking

All Scripture quotations, unless otherwise noted, are from The Holy Bible,
New International Version.

Library of Congress Cataloging-in-Publication Data

Bass, Charles D.
  Banishing fear from your life.

  1. Peace of mind—Religious aspects—Christianity.
2. Fear—Religious aspects—Christianity.   I. Title.
BV4908.5.B37   1986   241'.4   85-23943

Preface

Writing this book has largely been a private endeavor. On evenings and weekends at our quiet home overlooking the Shark River Basin, I worked on it over a two-year period. After the first draft, though, it abruptly became a public enterprise. I began to get unexpected help from numerous quarters. People would hear about it and ask to read the manuscript. Several offered highly valuable editorial comments, most of which were incorporated into later drafts. Some asked for copies to send to needy friends. A few generously provided distinctly professional assistance in preparing for publication. Each one seemed to take pride in making his or her contribution to what has ultimately become a kind of group project.

Also, the encouragement I received in many casual conversations has been helpful. I have been very astonished at how swiftly people have grasped the simple theme of the book and have promptly recounted stories from their own experiences validating the theme. It is as though I have been enabled to put into words a highly common but seldom discussed principle of life. The concept is not new, but the expression of it seems to be. Perhaps many readers will find in this book the intellectual framework for a procedure that can be effective in banishing all fear from their lives. Generally if we can describe a process, then we can repeat that process. I have tried to describe the process of banishing fear, and I fondly hope that many people can learn to repeat the process in their own lives.

For those who have both helped and encouraged me, I am profoundly grateful. I wish to acknowledge especially the painstaking criticism of Stan Russo, who for two years meticulously coached me to improve my communication. Similar criticism of the completed manuscript was graciously provided by Dr. Gerald G. Jampolsky, Marion ("Tiger") Meade, and C. Daniel Bass, my own son. The book might not even be in print today but for the expert professional help and advice offered by David Nimmo. Most helpful, with much daily support and loving encouragement, has been my dear wife, Martha. Together we rejoice to share this book with you as an expression of our love for you.

Wall, New Jersey

Contents

Foreword

It is significant that the first words recorded from man (Adam) in the Genesis account of the Creation included the phrase, "I was afraid." (Genesis 3:10) The capacity for fear has been both a blessing and a curse in humanity's experience from the very beginning.

For us to deal with the experience adequately and discover a freedom from its crippling effects on our lives, it is necessary to experience fear, probe its pain, and discover deliverance. Charles Bass has done this. In his military experience in jungle warfare, he faced his fears. He named them. He discovered the source of strength to overcome them. Later, he discovered the many faces of fear in everyday life and the adequacy of the strategy for overcoming both nameless dread and obvious threat. Now he turns to tell the rest of us on the journey some of the things he has found out about life and fear and God.

One of his most profound insights is that fear is at the root of so many other things with which we struggle. He says, "I have become convinced that no matter what the negative feeling you may have, you can peel back the layers and the last layer will be fear." If this thesis is true, then the overcoming of the basic emotion of fear and redirecting the adrenalin rush of that energy into positive and productive activity is very high on the agenda for finding fulfillment in life. Charles Bass points the way.

Reared in parsonages in small Texas towns, Bass's experience will speak to many who have grown up in some sense insulated from physical danger and then found themselves thrust into the jungles of our streets. There is no insulation these days for the fear of destruction from nuclear holocaust. Fear of pain and dread of suffering haunts us with every physical examination in a disease-filled world. Economic security has been held as a positive and achievable goal in our society. The uncertainties that face our economic future create a whole new wave of fear and apprehension in people's lives. Each of these pathways of life, which often generate paralyzing fears, is examined in the light of the new resources of the Spirit of God and the promises of the Word of God.

Books that offer magic-wand solutions to the complexities of our struggles can plunge us into deeper despair. Bass avoids this by dealing realistically with our fear and even more authentically with the presence of God he has discovered through his own experience. He shares with us a pattern for victory which needs to be taken seriously. His answers center not in the gyrations of manipulating our own mindset, but in the very presence and promise of God.

Dr. Jimmy Allen, President
American Christian Television System
Fort Worth, Texas

PART I

The Real Possibility of Banishing Fear

1

The Golden Possibility

Have you ever experienced a storm in a small boat? I did one summer, as a college student working between semesters with a seismograph crew in Texas. We were "shooting" Galveston Bay, which meant drilling beneath the bottom of the bay and exploding charges in order to record the vibrations and map out the underlying rock formations. I was the last one hired, so I served as roustabout and rotated among a variety of positions.

The day in question was my first day planting the dynamite. The procedure was for two men to maneuver a small motorboat out to a pipe protruding from the water and to lower a long canister of dynamite down into the pipe. My responsibility was to prepare the canister and lower it while the other man operated the skiff.

The day began beautifully. Through the morning we had little to do while the drill boat was planting the pipe. As we waited aboard the "shooting boat," I noticed a strange thing. The water had suddenly become very still! Placid! Like glass! All air motion had suddenly come to a halt. I looked up to see an ugly dark cloud moving quickly in from the west. It was during this quiet spell that we had to board our little boat to shoot the first hole. Since the distance to the pipe was only a couple of hundred feet, it seemed like a simple task; I busied myself positioning the cap into the canister as we rode along.

As soon as we pulled away from the larger boat, though, a fascinating display of tiny ripples began to form upon the glassy surface. A gentle wind had begun to blow. Gentle at first, but before we reached the pipe, a raging storm was in progress. Our little boat was bobbing furiously in and out of the deep troughs. As best we could, we proceeded with our mission, but I knew we were in serious trouble. While the operator valiantly tried to steer toward the pipe, I stood at the prow of the boat, grasping the explosive tightly in my hand.

"Grab onto the pipe!" he shouted.

I reached desperately but could not touch it. The sea was too rough.

"I can't," I shouted.

To add to our complications, lightning began. There I was, dynamite in one hand, holding on with the other, and standing in a boat loaded with explosives while lightning flashed all around.

"Then get that cap out of the canister!" shouted the operator.

Trembling with fright, I hastily withdrew the cap and carefully returned the dangerous articles to their containers. Then, spinning the skiff away from the wind, we dashed back to the mother boat. You can imagine how relieved I was to leave that little boat and watch it drift rapidly out to the end of its tether, only to hear the ominous statement, "There's enough dynamite in that boat to blow all our boats to smithereens." Fortunately, though, we waited out the rest of the storm without incident.

Perhaps the storm which Jesus and his disciples experienced on the Sea of Galilee came up just as suddenly and unexpectedly. Their cruise occurred at night; but surely if there had been any sign of a storm, these experienced fishermen would not have embarked. I doubt that they would have shared the fascination I had with the sudden calming of the sea, for they knew all too well what followed! With the same swiftness as the storm I encountered, a tremendous gale swept down on their frail craft. They had no mother ship to retreat to, as we had, and had to stand the full brunt of the storm alone. Within a short time their little ship was being swamped by the roaring waves. Tough hands flew to remove the sail and tackle and to bail out the threatening water. Alas, it seemed utterly hopeless. Where was the mighty Carpenter during all this? Incredibly he was lying upon a cushion in the stern of the boat. He had slept through it all! They even had to awaken him to apprise him of the danger.

"Master, Master, we're going to drown!" they shouted.[1]

Do you recall the rest of the story? Jesus awakened, spoke to the wind and water, and brought about an unbelievable calm.

We shall return to this story often as a model for the book's central theme, so I want us to analyze it carefully. Notice especially the first words of Jesus upon awakening: "You of little faith, why are you so afraid?" A simple question, but think of the implications behind it.

Jesus was literally charging the disciples with faulty emotional response, implying that their fear was inappropriate to the occasion. What is your opinion? Do you think their fear was appropriate or not? From all I have read in psychology, fear was the most appropriate response available in an event of such obvious danger. A psychologist would say their fear was perfectly normal, and indeed the lack of fear on such an occasion would have been more suspect than the fear itself.

Why then did Jesus find fault with their fear? The explanation lies in the way he addressed them, "You of little faith."[2] The positioning together of "fear" and "faith" in Jesus' remark is of major significance and explains his disappointment over their behavior. Observe the two questions[3] side by side: (a.) "Why are you so afraid?" (b.) "Where is your faith?" A causal relationship can be seen between the two sentences. If *a,* then *b:* "If you are so afraid, then you must have little faith."

I suggest to you that the incompatibility of fear and faith is a general principle of human behavior—a psychological phenomenon. You are less a person of faith when you are afraid than when you are unafraid. This is a truism; but fortunately we do not stop there. If you will read carefully, you can detect another implication even more revealing than the first. While fear may evidence a lack of faith, the reverse is also true. *FAITH CAN CONQUER FEAR!* Jesus was saying, "Why are you so afraid? Where is your faith? I can see that your faith was down to begin with, because if you had had faith, you would not have become frightened."

There is the exciting truth I have been building up to, the realization that one day changed my life. Can you see now why Jesus found their fear so inappropriate to the circumstances? He believed that faith had the power to subdue fear in any circumstance, even in this tremendous storm, so he deeply regretted his friends' failure to take advantage of it.

As we proceed, you will find this truth to be an important life principle, but one that has been long overlooked. Jesus intended for his disciples to learn it. Since then, it has been a principle available to people of all generations. The principle is that your faith can banish your fears. I caution you not to underestimate the significance of this. This is not a vague generalization nor some remote or future possibility. Christ did not mean that someday, when your faith grows so large, it will conquer your fear. Not at all! He meant that right now a specific fear that you have can be overcome by a specific faith. You can use faith as a coping device for fear.

My own discovery of this principle grew not so much out of my research as out of my personal experience. My long career as an Army chaplain has been filled with many fearful situations. A common saying in the Army is that "Courage is the soldier's virtue"—"courage" because a soldier's life is so filled with danger.

Although I believe that serious threats abound in virtually all vocations, there is that one threat which the military person faces that is unique to him—combat! The soldier lives, trains, dresses, and waits for combat. Though we are not engaged in it often, the thought of it is never far from our minds. I have personally been through combat and have tasted the full terrors of it. I have known raw, rash, naked fear, and I know it to be one of the most demoralizing experiences of human existence.

Nor are combat fears the only fears I have known. Like many others, I have been anxious about debts, employer reports, child rearing, disease, pain, and so forth. When it comes to the subject of fear, I speak out of broad experience.

For many years I carried the albatross of fear upon my back and struggled against it. Regrettably, no one ever taught me that I did not have to be afraid. Indeed, just the opposite. I was taught that I am afraid, and because I am, I must get in touch with my emotions. The implication was that if I got in touch with my fears, they would just go away. It was called coping with fears, "coping" meaning to do combat with. Others said that if I could come to understand my fears—understand what it is that I am afraid of or how my fears originated—they would go away. No one ever told me that it is unnecessary for me to fear at all. I had never before read an article or heard a speech that challenged the emotion of fear itself.

Nevertheless, somehow it began to dawn upon me that my biggest problems were not the things I feared but rather my fears themselves. Over time a hope began to emerge in me that I could learn to conquer fear itself. The more I thought about it, the more attractive this prospect became. If I could just banish the emotion of fear, I would nip the problem in the bud. I would not need to understand why I became afraid (which can often be a labyrinthian search) to be able to overcome fear. I would not even need to cope with or combat fear, for it would not be there to combat. Gradually, therefore, I began to direct my efforts toward the conquest of fear itself.

I can well remember how I finally succeeded in the quest for this serenity, this fearlessness, during the time of my second tour of duty in Germany. Generally it was an enjoyable, though long tour—thirty-nine solid months in length. The duty was no more difficult than normal, but admittedly the place had some peculiarities that heightened the stress upon the American population living there. The location, known as Miesau Army Depot, was a semiremote site, near the French border, cursed with an almost constant cloud cover. My wife swore the area bred its own clouds, for whenever we left Miesau, we always drove out from under the clouds; and when we returned, invariably we drove back under them. Many found the area depressing, and much of my ministry as a chaplain dealt with depression, drugs, alcohol, suicide, murder, child abuse, etc.

About midway of the tour I found myself immersed in an intense flow of counseling, programs, projects, visitations, and religious services that left a residue of tenseness and heaviness within me. One day my commander addressed me among a small group of individuals outside his office and said, "Chaplain, you look worried."

"Sir, I feel quite burdened," I admitted and left it at that. But it felt strange to be the recipient of the kind of encouragement I was so much more accustomed to giving than receiving.

It was during those hectic days that I experienced a most remarkable awakening. I had driven home from the depot for lunch one day and was returning alone in my old black Merce-des. I can distinctly remember how the understanding of Jesus' words to the disciples in the boat suddenly blossomed in my mind: "You of little faith, why are you so afraid?" A light dawned within me, giving me the clear understanding that "faith can conquer fear." I felt at that moment as though a veil had been lifted from my mind. In leaps and bounds I raced across my mental store of Biblical knowledge, confirming in innumerable ways this simple truth: "Faith can conquer fear." For the rest of that day I felt as light-hearted as a child on a playground as I mulled over the clarity of this newfound concept. The freshness of it never faded, and I went through the balance of that tour with a lessened tension and a most welcomed calmness.

Since then I have experimented with this formula in real life time and again, yet never have I known it to fail. I had discovered literally how to conquer fear. Oh, I still get apprehensive from time to time, but there is this difference: Now I have the key. Now I know how to suppress fears in all circumstances. It works!

The force of this concept may not hit you at first. The truth of it is so plain and simple; and yet somehow it has to ignite within you. That is why I have dedicated a book to it: to explore it thoroughly and hopefully to strike some sparks. The golden possibility is that you and I can be free of fear. Just imagine—no more fears!

NOTES

1. *Luke* 8:24
2. *Matthew* 8:26
3. *Matthew* 8:26, "You of little faith, why are you so afraid?" *Mark* 4:40, "Why are you so afraid? Do you still have no faith?" *Luke* 8:25, "Where is your faith?"

2
Imagine! No More Fears

In this chapter I shall try to unfold for you what this discovery has meant to me personally and what I believe it can mean to anyone. What I discovered was basically a solution to the problem of my own fearfulness. *Before* my discovery, I would feel fear over a variety of different experiences. *After,* very few things have caused me any significant fear. As I write these words, they seem so inadequate in expressing the depth of relief I felt in being set free from those fears, for I experienced a very profound emotional change. I attribute this change entirely to my discovery of this formula. When I describe my experience as a profound emotional change, however, I do not mean that it was like a conversion experience, in which once I was fearful but now am courageous. Rather it was more like learning a new process or a new technique. Suppose that I had played golf all my life but all along had been a very poor golfer. Then one day an instructor said to me, "Your problem is that your hands are placed wrong on the golf club. Your left hand should be above your right hand, not the way you've been doing it." So I could say that ever since that lesson my golf game has been revolutionized because I have been applying my new technique. In the same way, what I have learned about the conquest of fear has been basically a technique or a mental hygiene process. Now, by applying my newfound technique, I am continually conquering my fears as they arise.

I believe also that anyone can learn this process and achieve one hundred percent conquest of his or her fears. The conquest of fear by faith is a universal formula. I have had many growth experiences in my life that would not necessarily be universal. If you were to experience them, you might achieve the same results I did; but then again you might not. I am confident, though, that if you apply faith to your fears, you will certainly conquer them the same way I have. In the golf illustration the lesson about the proper placement of hands on the club is a universal lesson. Anyone who places his left hand above his right hand (provided he is right-handed) will hit the ball better than if he reversed his hands. Now the golf instructor might have taught me many other lessons that would have also improved my golf game, but that would not have been universal—lessons about my stance, my eye movement, my swing. These techniques applied to me only and might not fit other people, but the technique of hand placement would apply to anyone.

I consider the potential for the conquest of fear by faith to be very far-reaching. I believe that by faith anyone can completely subdue momentary fear, latent fear, recurring fear, free-floating fear, or any other kind of fear in his or her life. I believe that the moment a person exercises faith, God will reach down inside that individual when he or she is afraid and remove all feelings of fear, just as a surgeon removes cancer. I believe that you can carry the cure for fear with you wherever you go—namely, faith. I believe that one who exercises faith continually will not even feel the emotion of fear. I believe, therefore, that a person can live a life without any fear in it.

From a psychological viewpoint, I am aware of the broad significance of these claims. Psychologists diagnose, essentially, four different emotions among humans: joy, sorrow, anger, and fear. All the feelings we ever have are included in one or the other of these categories, and we all experience each of them at one time or another. Now if the category of fear were removed, our human psyche would be radically changed. Ideally that is the golden possibility that faith can achieve in a life!

Surely no one can deny that the removal of fear would be a most welcome change. We may say that the loss of certain characteristics would make us less than human, but if we lost fear there would be no such complaint. To lose fear would be to lose the negative of life, the anchor, the deadweight. I call fear the "negative" of "positive thinking," the "impossibility" of "possibility thinking." I believe that virtually all negative emotions are contained within fear. Would it not leave a life of joy, hope, and love if you never again experienced fear?!

I must make one further explanation about my personal experience. I did not discover the principle of faith conquering fear purely out of trial and error; I did not just exercise faith toward one of my fears one day and say, "Aha! it works!" No, I first discovered it as a recorded principle in the Bible. That is to say, the rational preceded the emotional, rather than vice versa. That day in Germany, I had been pondering the words of Jesus in the boat when it suddenly hit me what he was saying. It was after I had made that realization that I deliberately tried the principle on some of my fears and found it to work. Since then, I have found the same principle revealed throughout the Bible. For example, the Psalmist David said, "I sought the Lord and he answered me; he delivered me from all my fears."[1] Isaiah echoed David in saying, "I will trust and not be afraid."[2] The process for Isaiah was the same process enunciated by Jesus: faith conquering fear.

The problem of fear within human beings is given special treatment in the Bible. Fear is part of the human predicament. Human fear began as a result of the first sin in the Garden of Eden when Adam confessed (in his first recorded words to God), "I was afraid."[3] The writer of *Hebrews* spoke of human beings as being slaves to fear.[4] In a very real sense Jesus came to liberate human beings from their captivity to fear.

Jesus' intent in teaching the disciples how to conquer fear was aimed at eliminating the deepest root of trouble within human existence. He cherished for people the very highest blessings: encouragement, joy, victory, success, inspiration. His desires for us necessitated taking something from us as well as giving something to us, or else his most cherished ambitions would be frustrated. To give to us joy, he must take away fear, for fear is the enemy of all joy, peace, and happiness. Joy and fear cannot be experienced simultaneously. Since fear prevents joy, it must be eradicated!

Jesus treated fear so seriously as to sum up all negative experiences in the single emotion of fear. Once a prominent leader named Jairus begged Jesus to come and heal his twelve-year-old daughter, who was dying.[5] Jesus accommodated him by going with him toward his home. En route, however, Jesus allowed himself to be delayed by another case of healing. He dawdled, as they say in Texas. Jairus meekly waited without interrupting, but you can imagine what he was feeling. Indeed his worst fears seemed to be confirmed when, as he waited, a messenger approached him and told him it was too late. "Your daughter is dead," he said. "Don't bother the teacher any more." Quickly, though, Jesus turned toward Jairus to help. (To Jairus such must have seemed like the Master's tardy interest in a case he had momentarily forgotten.) Alas it was too late! Yet Jesus spoke directly to Jairus, "Don't be afraid. Just believe, and she will be healed." Surely enough, she was healed.

Pay special attention to those words, "Don't be afraid!" They are so similar to his words to the disciples in the boat. At first glance, however, fear does not appear to have been what Jairus was feeling at the moment. Clearly, rather, he was experiencing grief or sorrow. And yet here was Jesus counseling him not to fear instead of encouraging him not to be sorrowful. Is it possible that to Jesus sorrow was a type of fear—that the cure for fear was also the cure for grief? Perhaps so! In support of this, notice the same juxtaposition of fear and faith that Jesus had stated in the boat with the implied promise that faith could conquer grief too. Earlier we said that sorrow, along with fear, is one of the four cardinal emotions; but here sorrow is practically equated with fear. Here is further confirmation that almost all negative emotions are contained within fear.

Let us try to imagine how fear encompasses all the negative feelings of life. Maybe it is like peeling back the leaves of an onion. You peel back the leaf of sorrow and beneath it, perhaps, is regret. You peel back regret and there is self-centeredness. You peel back self-centeredness and, perhaps, there is doubt. You peel back doubt and there, lo, is fear, perhaps the fear of loneliness. I have become convinced that no matter what the negative feeling you may have, you can peel back the layers and the last layer will be fear.

I have confirmed this fact many times in my own life. When I first put into practice the cure-by-faith method, I was applying it only to circumstances in which I was clearly afraid. How excited I was when I discovered it worked! I started using it more. My fears were getting knocked over like pins in a bowling alley. I found myself rebounding from fright with an astonishing resiliency (astonishing to me, at least). Soon I was applying the method to any and all fears that came along. I became so enthusiastic that before I was aware of it, I was practicing it on other negative emotions, emotions I would not normally call fear. For example, if my feelings got hurt because someone else was receiving preferential treatment over me, I would no longer just chide myself for jealousy. Yes, I would still do that, but I would also pray, "Lord, strengthen my faith and take away my fears." It worked! To this day I cannot explain how fear is a part of jealousy or a part of grief or a part of frustration, although I believe that it is. But I have found fear somehow to be involved in all negative feelings. Fear stands out as the deadliest of all our emotions. Therefore, the miracle of the victory of faith over fear is magnified all the more.

Would it not be pleasant to be free of fear? It can happen to you too, and then you will be able to shout, "Free, free, free at last!" Perhaps Jesus was talking about freedom from fear when he said, "If the Son sets you free, you will be free indeed."[6]

NOTES

1. *Psalm* 34:4
2. *Isaiah* 12:2
3. *Genesis* 3:10
4. *Hebrews* 2:15
5. *Luke* 8:40–56
6. *John* 8:36

3

Banishing Fear Means Banishing Fear's Offspring

How certain negative emotions are contained within fear may be a mystery, but the relationship of others is obvious. They are contained within fear because they grow directly out of fear. It is of these by-products of fear that I wish to speak now.

A glorious possibility exists concerning these emotions as it does concerning the emotion of fear. The conquest of our fears means the conquest of these emotions too. All these by-products of fear may be successfully removed by the same process that removes our fears—the process of faith. So the potential of the cure-by-faith method shall commend itself to our judgment more persuasively, more thoroughly, and more dramatically for each new target toward which we aim it.

ANXIETY

The first target is anxiety. I do not intend to write a lengthy treatise on anxiety—there are already enough such works that deplore the amount of anxiety in our society today—but simply to demonstrate that when you learn to conquer fear, you can conquer anxiety too. God's word clearly commands, "Do not be anxious about anything."[1]

Consider how anxiety is related to fear—how anxiety grows out of fear and includes fear as its principal ingredient. What exactly is anxiety? It is the feeling of apprehension over some impending or anticipated threat. Two words in this definition distinguish anxiety from ordinary fear: the words "impending" and "anticipated." Both words have the flavor of a future, not a present, occurrence. The threat has not yet materialized, but we believe it is going to do so. On the other hand, ordinary fear applies to things present and tangible, to occurrences that are already happening.

This characteristic of worrying about the future is one of the hallmarks of our present age. The degree of our anxiety is almost unprecedented in history, and it corresponds to the unprecedented decline of our faith. The media frequently borrowed W. H. Auden's phrase "the age of anxiety" to describe the seventies. The peculiar aspect of the modern world is not the gravity of its contemporary problems so much as it is the gloom over its anticipated problems. Paradoxically we are not as worried about the difficulties we are actually experiencing as we are about the disasters that have not yet happened—and may never happen. For example, we are anxious that excessive fluorocarbons from spray cans will damage the ozone layer. We are disturbed over the depletion of natural resources. If population and technology keep growing at the present rate, we expect that world conditions will deteriorate. Overpopulation with catastrophic food shortages will ensue. Pollution will damage our health, alter the climate, and ruin the atmosphere. Inflation will continue, unemployment will spread, the recession will return, and the world economy will collapse. Another depression will emerge. Terrorism will increase. And of course standing in the wings as a constant source of anxiety is the threat of nuclear war.

In one section of the Sermon on the Mount[2], Jesus addressed this tendency to worry about the future. He concluded the section with these words: "Therefore do not worry about tomorrow, for tomorrow will worry about itself. Each day has enough trouble of its own." I think he was saying something like this, "Don't waste emotional energy worrying about tomorrow. When tomorrow comes, there will be enough people concerned about its troubles to solve them then. In the meantime save your emotional energy and apply it to current problems."

We have all seen people so distracted by their fear of the future that they neglect today's responsibilities. Do you think they intended to do this? Not really. Likely none of them said, "I'm going to quit working so I can have time to worry!" What happens? They worry with such intensity that they do not have the energy left for normal endeavors. It is almost as though a person possesses only enough emotional energy for one day at a time. We are allotted only one day's basic load of ammunition. If we expend it on tomorrow's problems, we do not have enough for today. Like manna in the wilderness, we can gather enough only for one day at a time.

The golden possibility is that you do not need to be anxious about tomorrow! I bid you pause for just a moment and take in that prospect. Your tomorrow will be okay. Do not worry about it. If your Bible is open to Jesus' words on anxiety in *Matthew* 6:25–34, note the many encouragements to your confidence. Your food, drink, and clothing will be provided. Life's necessities will be met; that you can count on. Life will be good to you. Depend on it. It always will be.

Like fuel for fire, Jesus is supplying content for faith all throughout this passage. Remember that faith conquers fear. Notice again the juxtaposition of faith and fear. Very reminiscent of his words in the boat, Jesus says here, "And why do you worry . . . O you of little faith?"[3]

STRESS

"Stress syndrome" is the name given to a wide range of biological phenomena being evidenced in this century. Over twenty million people in this country have high blood pressure. About the same number are alcoholics. Nearly thirty-five percent of all deaths are due to heart attacks. The abuse of drugs is the eleventh leading cause of death. Twenty-five to fifty thousand people a year commit suicide. These and many other similar health hazards comprise the stress syndrome.

Stress is any change in our body, usually negative, resulting from any demand that may be put upon us. Some of the more dramatic physical effects attributable to stress include atherosclerosis, strokes, angina pectoris, heart attacks, hypertension, ulcers, diabetes, and migraine headaches. Because today certain common physical disorders, such as asthma, are being traced to a breakdown in our immune system, these too are suspected to arise from stress. This means that your allergies, viruses, flus, and colds may result from stress. The immune system is now suspect as a causative factor in cancer, so that even some cancer may be the result of stress!

Can it be that such dread diseases as I have mentioned are, so to speak, self-inflicted wounds? If they are the products of stress, that would appear to be the case. You see, stress is not something that happens to us from the outside; it is something we bring upon ourselves.

Someone may object and say: I do not agree. Stress is *not* something we bring upon ourselves; it is a product of our environment. We live in one of the most stressful eras in history. I believe that the rapid change we are experiencing today—the "future shock"—is what is taking its toll upon the human body.

This is not what the experts are saying. Although they acknowledge that the environment does impact upon us, they label those impacts as "stressors," not stress. They reserve the label "stress" for the body's response to those exterior events. The fact is that there is an intermediary between the stressor and the bodily reaction. It is the mind. How your mind views that stressor is the factor that determines whether your body will react to it in a maladaptive way. You might say that it is your own mind that determines whether a certain event shall in fact be a stressor or not.

How is fear associated with stress? Modern psychological theory puts fear at the very origin of stress. An earlier theory postulated by Walter Cannon and known as the "fight/flight syndrome" has been adapted to fit stress theory. Early man, Cannon said, who lived in more direct communion with nature, was frequently confronted with life-threatening situations. For example, a nomad squatting comfortably in his camp may suddenly see a lion approaching. Immediately the man must fight or take flight for his life. Immediately and instinctively his body prepares him for either option. His pupils dilate to allow more light to enter. His muscles tense in preparation for strenuous action. His breath rate shoots up, providing more oxygen. Stored sugar and fats pour into his bloodstream to provide fuel for quick energy. Biologically these changes are the components of stress. Scientists say that this adaptive system served early man well, but today the same mechanism becomes self-destructive. Here is the reason.

Modern man usually cannot effectively come down off the biological high this syndrome produces within his body. If a big truck were to run a stop sign in front of you, causing you to swerve dangerously to avoid a major catastrophe, the incident would probably trigger the same biological changes within your body as the nomad experienced when confronted by the lion. The nomad could have worked off his tension immediately by fighting or fleeing (provided of course that he outran or outfought the lion). You, however, have no such options and are left with a bundle of tension and no way to discharge it. Such stress takes its toll in wear and tear on your body. Research has shown that the fight/flight syndrome of changes also results from threatening situations that may not be so immediate and direct as the truck incident. If you were to go into work tomorrow and the president of your company were to tell you he was thinking of moving your division to Panama, the fight/flight syndrome might immediately begin within you.

The fight/flight syndrome upon which stress is based is nothing other than fear. Therefore, the golden possibility is that stress can be effectively prevented by the conquest of fear. Perhaps the tell-tale sign of fear that Jesus saw in the faces of the disciples when he woke up in the boat was their dilated pupils, one of the typical stress reactions. His implied promise of the conquest of fear was addressed to us in a classic fight/flight situation. His message to us is that if faith could conquer fear in a situation where the threat was direct and immediate and where the reaction was instinctive, spontaneous and automatic, how much more easily could it conquer fear in situations where we have the leisure for reflection, meditation, and prayer? If Jesus were to speak to us today, he might ask, "You of little faith, why are you in stress?"

ANGER

Another offspring of fear might be anger. Not always is this the case, but when anger is produced by fear, the cure-by-faith method can apply to anger too. The process by which fear provokes anger is relatively simple: we use anger to cope with fear.

I once counseled a middle-aged couple who interacted with a fear/anger reaction. Privately the husband told me, "Everytime I come home, Mary is waiting for me with a chip on her shoulder. I hate to go home. As I drive home, I get more and more tense. When I get home and see her waiting for me with her hands on her hips, it just makes me mad, and I tie into her before she can get the jump on me."

Mary in turn confided to me privately, "Joe is always mad at me over something. He frightens me sometimes. He always comes home in a bad temper. I really have to stand up to him to defend myself."

Both partners had lost faith. Neither believed in the love of the other, and neither had faith that God could love him or her through the partner. If she had exercised faith, she would have felt God was caring for her and would not have feared so much her partner's withholding of love. Nor would he have expressed such anger had he felt confident that God would continue to love him no matter how she interacted with him. Consequently each could have acted in a more relaxed, confident manner.

DEPRESSION

Tied closely to the emotion of anger is the state of depression. Common theory states that depression occurs because anger is repressed. So if this anger were the product of fear, then depression too would be an expression of fear. Numbers of authors today diagnose depression to be a symptom of anxiety. The decline into depression may take several routes. One may become fearful or anxious over something. Priding himself in his resourcefulness and self-confidence, he becomes distressed over his fearfulness, becoming angry with himself over the awareness that he is afraid. Thus he sinks into depression. Or one may become angry first and fearful second. Having become angered, he may be fearful of expressing his anger. He may be angry with his employer but fearful of expressing it. Or the anger may not fit a public image he or she has so carefully cultivated or the image he holds of himself. So he becomes depressed as a defense against emotions he does not want to recognize within himself. Most theories hold that depression results somehow from an individual becoming angry with himself.

The cure-by-faith method can be an effective preventative of depression. First, a person of faith is one who has learned to correctly identify fear within himself. Knowing that fear is the enemy and destroyer of his faith, he learns to identify his enemy in order to protect his faith. No general would ignore a contingent of enemy troops roving freely throughout his area of operations. Rather he puts out highly sensitive information collectors seeking to trace the movements of his enemy at all times. He seeks to know his enemy as well as he knows his own troops. So we are to be ever vigilant against our fears, expectantly awaiting them to raise their heads, not in order that we may deny them but that we may destroy them by means of faith. Many people, to their own hurt, are denying their fears, a self-defeating tactic in warfare.

The cure-by-faith method can also be an effective healer of depression, even after it sets in. Choosing deliberately to have faith (for faith *is* always one of his options), the depressed person probes his consciousness for all faith-denying fears. As irradiated iodine injected into the bloodstream automatically seeks out all thyroid tissues in the body to destroy them, so your faith can trace all fears and effectively neutralize them.

TIMIDITY

A timid person is one unusually affected by fear. Being afraid of public opinion, he is afraid to express himself openly. Bible commentators believe no less a celebrity than Timothy was subject to timidity. A careful exegesis of the New Testament suggests that Timothy's mentor, the apostle Paul, exerted subtle influence upon his protégé in an attempt to lift the level of his self-confidence.[4] To be sure, if you are basically timid, you stand in good company.

This is not to say that a cure for timidity is intended to produce cockiness, arrogance, or overconfidence. Such would be contrary to the Christian principle of humility. Frequently Paul implied he also had feelings of self-doubt. He seemed to evidence a strange mixture of both confidence and timidity: confidence in God but distrust of himself. A fine line exists here. The cure-by-faith method is not designed to create self-confidence *per se* within an individual. In the boat Jesus was not striving to engender self-confidence within the disciples—not self-confidence but God-confidence. The faith operative in cure-by-faith is not faith in self but faith in God.

Paul seemed to take pride in Timothy, but Timothy's timidity was not one of his assets. Nor is it an asset in you or me. It needs to be dealt with and cured. Note that it was to Timothy that Paul addressed the significant statement, "For God did not give us a spirit of timidity but a spirit of power, of love, and of self-discipline."[5] To cure timidity—and it does need to be cured—recognize it as the fear it is and cure it by faith.

EMBARRASSMENT

Another product of fear—one that may be associated with timidity—is embarrassment. To be embarrassed is to be rendered painfully self-conscious. Its hallmarks are a flushed face and a mildly confused state of mind. Normally it occurs unexpectedly, quickly, and spontaneously. One recovers from it rather rapidly. Basically it represents a moment when one is acutely fearful of public opinion. It is a passing apprehension that others will not think well of you, will subject you to ridicule, or will censor you. As a major emotion, embarrassment has little significance other than in what it may reveal about the individual. Because the embarrassed reaction is so spontaneous, others may interpret it to be a true indication of a hidden aspect of oneself. It may be thought to be a sign of weakness or self-doubt. Certainly it is proof that one places a high premium upon the public's opinion of oneself.

As with the experience of the disciples in the boat, embarrassment happens too rapidly for one to cope with or effectively control. When one is caught with his pants down, as the saying goes, it is too late for him to reason within himself and ask, "What other options to a red face do I have in this situation?" Only one action can prevent embarrassment: prior preparation. Faith still cures fear, but in this case it must be faith in advance. Beginning the day with some exercise of faith, such as prayer, Bible study, or meditation, can effectively prepare one for any eventuality, expected or unexpected. Did you know that there is a promise you can claim which assures you that you will not be embarrassed when you have faith? "Everyone who trusts in him will never be put to shame."[6] Pray as an old deacon prayed, "Lord, prepare us for what thou art preparing for us." Such an exercise of faith performed daily should keep your mind in a frame of reference that prefers to please God rather than men. Faith would keep you aware that the primary audience before whom you are performing is divine, not human. So to prevent the occurrence of embarrassment, take in advance "the shield of faith with which you can extinguish all the flaming arrows of the evil one."[7]

SELF-FULFILLING DREAD

The phenomenon known as self-fulfilling dread is another offspring of fear that can be eliminated by faith. Occasionally by a strange mental quirk, people actually bring to pass events they deeply dread. For example, I know an Army officer and his wife who were very apprehensive about his going to work for a certain supervisor. When they were preparing to move to the new assignment, we talked together, and both aired their suspicions that he would be treated unfairly when he got there. Later I heard, as a matter of fact, that he did get a poor rating. Both the rater and the ratee were personal friends of mine, so when I saw the rater again, I asked what were the circumstances that brought on the poor rating. He told how the officer had been uncooperative and resistant to his leadership. His wife, especially, had publically condemned the rater, had charged him with unfairness, and in various other ways had demonstrated animosity and hostility against him personally. He concluded, "I had no choice but to rate him marginally." I believe he brought this misfortune on himself in a classic case of self-fulfilling dread.

Perhaps in more innocuous ways, we all have at one time or

another provoked some unfortunate experience simply because we were afraid such an experience might one day happen to us. The process of dread-fulfillment is seldom clearcut, and the victim may never be aware he brought it on himself. It is a form of self-fulfilling prophecy and may happen quite frequently.

Dr. Vance Havner, long-time Christian speaker and author, tells a humorous little story that illustrates self-fulfilling dread. A hillbilly accidentally wandered into a cemetery one night. When he realized where he was, he got out of there in record time, stumbling over tombstones, falling down, scratching himself in the bushes. The next morning someone asked him, "Don't you know that a ghost can't hurt you?"

"I know that," he replied, "but they can sure make you hurt yourself."[8]

Fear can sure make us hurt ourselves.

The cure for dread-fulfillment is a preventive one: just avoid the feeling of dread in the first place. Put your faith to work and conquer fear by faith. Faith, as we will see later, has a way of expecting good, not bad, to happen to us. By exercising faith, one can tap the power of self-fulfilling prophecy for his benefit rather than his detriment. He can predict good things to happen to him and thereby contribute to their happening. The above officer and his wife could possibly have changed their fate by exercising an attitude of trust. If the man could not trust the supervisor, he at least could have trusted God. He could have had faith that God would protect him from whatever threat an unfair supervisor might pose. "If God is for us, who can be against us?"[9] You have every right to be optimistic about your future if you have faith in God. You can expect the very best to happen to you. As William Carey said, "Expect great things from God."

NOTES

1. *Philippians* 4:6
2. *Matthew* 6:25
3. *Matthew* 6:25–34
4. *1 Corinthians* 15:10
5. *2 Timothy* 1:7

6. *Romans* 10:11
7. *Ephesians* 6:16
8. Vance Havner, *Jesus Only* (Old Tappan, N.J.: Revell, 1969), p. 80
9. *Romans* 8:31

4
Wasted Fears

People have odd and divergent reactions to what I call "wasted emotions." Wasted emotions are those emotions that are eventually proven by circumstances to have been unnecessary to the occasion. Such emotions may be either pleasant or unpleasant, and we tend to evaluate the unpleasant ones differently from the pleasant ones.

For example, a pleasant emotion may be the sensation of joy one feels in anticipating some pleasant event. A young lady may be invited on a date by a man who excites her tremendously. All day long she primps and prepares herself, all the while floating on cloud nine. For some reason, however, when the time of the date arrives, the man does not. He stands her up. All her girl friends gather round her and naturally criticize the man profusely for building up her hopes and then standing her up. Of course they judge it to have been better had he not invited her at all than to have invited her and stood her up.

My observation is that we tend to frown upon the pleasant wasted emotion. We pity the person for her temporary hope. The poet cannot convince us it is better to have loved and lost than never to have loved at all. This same observation applies to most pleasant wasted emotions.

On the other hand, we have no such criticism for the unpleasant wasted emotion. For example, one person discovers an unexpected lump in his body. He becomes greatly alarmed, fearing cancer. He becomes moody and touchy and slips into depression. People gather around him and try to cheer him up, but everyone sympathizes with him, thoroughly understanding the reason he feels as he does. He goes to a doctor, however, and discovers that the tumor was benign. Minor surgery removes it, and he quickly bounces back to his former cheerfulness. Yet no one thinks to pity him for his wasted depression or declares it a shame that he spent all that moodiness for nothing.

Now observe the contrast. We condemn the wasted pleasant emotion but complacently accept the wasted unpleasant emotion. We judge it altogether regrettable that one should have experienced a hope that later came to nought but understandable and appropriate that one should experience a fear that later also came to nought. Why are we not more logical? Why not praise the good emotion—it was very pleasant while it lasted—and pity the bad emotion—it was so sad to experience all that mental pain for nothing?

The wasted unpleasant emotion is a very frequent occurrence, so frequent as to require the formulation of some remedy. I think it occurs more often than we realize. Whenever relief does come for it, we rejoice so much that we do not think to look back. We say something about it being just so much spilt milk and scarcely question whether we could have prevented the unpleasant emotion anyway. Could we indeed have prevented it? Think about that question, for prevention could possibly be the remedy we are searching for. If the wasted unpleasant emotion is as frequent as we believe it to be, then something needs to be done to prevent it from happening in the first place. For example, we deal with anger in a preventive manner; we say, "Count to ten before you get angry." I suggest we can deal with fear in a similar manner.

We have seen how the fear of the disciples in the boat turned out to be wasted emotion. The story's conclusion reveals that they had nothing to fear. If only they had known! Like us, they would not have given the wasting of their fears a second thought if Jesus had not forcibly brought it to their attention. I challenge you, the reader, to reflect upon the many times your situation turned out so much better than you feared it would. Think about all the fear you have wasted on airplane flights that landed safely, job interviews that turned out well, stage fright that preceded your most successful performances, or needless anxiety over finances, friends, children, sports, or examinations. All of it counted for tons of wasted gastric juices, wasted adrenaline, and wasted fears.

The point is that faith is capable of preventing the occurrence of wasted fear. It is unnecessary for you to experience inappropriate fear in the first place. Such is the implication of Jesus' words, "You of little faith, why are you so afraid?" I suggest five reasons why fear should not be wasted.

1. FOR REALITY THINKING. Fear should not be wasted, first, because most things we fear never materialize. As an indicator of what the future holds, fear has a very poor batting average. Our fears are extremely deceptive, often convincing us of gross unreality. *Ecclesiastes* describes how "men rise up at the sound of birds,"[1] a paranoid reaction. *Proverbs* says:

> The wicked man flees, though no one pursues. But the righteous are as bold as a lion.[2]

Worry is one of the biggest deceivers of all, yet many defend it. Those of us who advocate nonworry are compared to Pollyanna. An unfriendly cartoonist in Jesus' day might have caricatured him as Alfred E. Newman of *Mad* magazine with his gleeful remark, "What? Me worry?" But the pessimism behind much worry is a judgment not based on facts. It is popular today to be pessimistic, negative, lowering, and hopeless; but this is a subjective call based on fear, not an objective call based upon reality. Why, the world we live in offers us great grounds for optimism. We have the best education, transportation, government, housing, food, possessions, entertainment, churches, and medicine in all history. Natural beauty is still existent and more accessible to the general public than ever before. The sun still shines, delicious food abounds, great music resounds, goodness thrives. Despite all the public opinion to the contrary today, the valid inference of a logical mind can be that life is wonderful. In reality, it is unnecessary for anyone to keep on worrying. Facts do not support a need for worry. Not one person on earth is born to worry. You are playing a false tape if you keep saying, "I'm a born worrier." You do not have to worry. No one does.

2. FOR CONSERVATION. Conservation today is a strong economic and political platform. Waste is publicly condemned, whether of energy, timber, wildlife, or other natural resources. Actually anxiety is one of our biggest wastes of all. People have wasted an exorbitant amount of fear over concerns that have never materialized, as, for instance, nuclear war. Millions have lived and died worrying over a conflagration that never happened in their lifetimes, all of them squandering their precious fears wantonly. Modern science has shown that the physical apparatus by which we experience fear is like a high-powered, premium-fueled, gas-guzzling machine. It costs energy, time, and health. Recently news personnel began observing the waning appearance of one of our nation's most prominent ladies. When they inquired about her health, she explained her condition by saying she had been worrying a lot lately but added that she was simply a natural worrier. Fear costs wear and tear.

3. TO AVOID DUPLICATION. An old proverb says, "He who fears death dies a thousand deaths." The fear of an event is like the duplication of that event; but if you do not fear it, it happens only once. This becomes another important reason for not wasting fears.

A challenging verse was given to a church in Asia Minor: "Do not be afraid of what you are about to suffer."[3] How interesting! I have been to the dentist quite often for some pretty extensive dental work. From the very first visit I have dreaded the dentist's office. As a child I once completely ducked an appointment because of fear, and I am still paying the price today. On my way to the office I would tense up, and in the waiting room I would break out in a cold sweat. In the chair minutes seemed like hours as my total attention focused on the doctor's every move. I suffered as much from fear as I did from pain. Fortunately those days are long gone, thanks to faith thinking. Although the dental work is just as painful today, the element of fear is no longer there. Thanks be to God for the grace of faith!

4. BECAUSE OF FUTURE GRACE. Fear should not be wasted because fear discounts the possibility of special grace in future trials. A faith thinker will avoid saying of some experience, "I could never go through that." "But it's true," someone objects, "I went to pieces the last time it happened, so I know." Be careful not to trap yourself in the past. Dr. Gerald G. Jampolsky, a California medical doctor, warns against holding rigidly to our old belief system: "So the fearful past becomes a fearful future, and the past and the future become one."[4] You cannot effectively judge the future by the past.

We truly do not know how victoriously we could go through a trial because we do not know how well God will strengthen us when that trial comes. The faith thinker believes that God will give special strength whenever a trial comes. This individual may not have that strength now, but he or she will have it when needed. The faith thinker does not anticipate any event with fear because his or her trust is in promises such as these:

As thy days, so shall thy strength be.[5]

God is faithful; he will not let you be tempted beyond what you can bear. But when you are tempted, he will also provide a way out so that you can stand up under it.[6]

But he gives us more grace.[7]

I remember an occasion as a young man when I felt as though I were undergoing an unfair experience. I resented very greatly that all this should be happening to me, for it seemed so much greater than anything my peers had to suffer. I cried out, "Why me, Lord?" I read the above verse from *1 Corinthians* 10:13, and it dawned upon me that if God would not allow temptations beyond our strength, then my strength must be above average, since my test was above average. I came to see it as a backhanded compliment and actually felt comforted by the thought. Looking back, I can see how much my ego was involved in the incident— even in the experience of comfort. Today I understand more clearly that the strength I had at the time was just a temporary loan to me from above and was not my innate strength. Nevertheless I believe all the more firmly today that if another experience like that comes along, I shall again be strengthened to bear it. You truly may not be able to bear some trials with the strength you now have, but when that heavy trial comes, sufficient strength will come along with it.

5. BECAUSE OF THE REWARD THAT IS COMING. Great effort is necessary to some accomplishments, and some degree of suffering seems necessary to certain rewards. To be free from my toothache, I had to make one painful trip to the dentist's office. Deep down inside I felt it was worth the trip. As a general rule I believe some good will come out of anything the believer suffers—if not here, then in the hereafter. That one thought can comfort the sufferer. For that reason you do not need to fear even the bad experience that lies ahead for you, for it will have a meaning, a purpose, and a reward. Of Moses it was said, "He regarded disgrace for the sake of Christ as of greater value than the treasurers of Egypt, because he was looking ahead to his reward."[8] When the fearful moment comes for you, try to imagine the reward in store for you. It will be worth it all. You will be able one day to look back and say, "I'm glad it happened to me." In the midst of the experience, keep your eye upon the reward.

NOTES

1. *Ecclesiastes* 12:4
2. *Proverbs* 28:1
3. *Revelation* 2:10
4. Gerald G. Jampolsky, *Love Is Letting Go of Fear* (Toronto: Bantam Books, 1981), p. 111
5. *Deuteronomy* 33:25 (KJV)
6. *1 Corinthians* 10:13
7. *James* 4:6
8. *Hebrews* 11:26

5

Encouraging Words

Before we leave this section on fear, I wish to demonstrate that your deliverance from fear is indeed one of the Bible's main objectives. Some readers may be encouraged to know that release from fear is a hope offered all through the Bible, not just in a limited portion. From my reading of it, I am thoroughly persuaded that such a hope is the very will of God for us. God does not want humans to be afraid, and so the fears we experience are emotions that are foreign to the purpose for which he created us. Undoubtedly we were not made to be afraid. One phrase, which is quoted as the direct words of God, crops up so repeatedly in the sacred book as to convince us of God's deep sympathy toward our fears. It is the phrase, "Fear not." I shall devote this chapter to expositions of passages where this encouraging message is repeated.

In the very first book it is addressed to the patriarch Abraham: "Do not be afraid, Abram. I am your shield, your very great reward."[1] If there is a promise to you and me enclosed in these words, it is the assurance that we are being protected, yes, shielded from harm. The promise of God's protection can become one of the main truths we believe in, the cornerstone of our fear-conquering faith.

Read also the message to Isaiah:

Do not call conspiracy everything that these people call conspiracy; do not fear what they fear, and do not dread it. The Lord Almighty is the one you are to regard as holy, he is the one you are to fear, he is the one you are to dread . . . I will wait for the Lord, who is hiding his face from the house of Jacob. I will put my trust in him.[2]

Did you notice that we are cautioned not to be afraid of something simply because other people are afraid of it? In other words, do not let yourself be infected by other people's fears. Fright can be contagious. We can become hooked by others' fears. Mass psychology can rule our emotions. I think subconsciously we reason that when a large number of people fear something, such an object is worthy of our fear too. Watch out, for such is the kind of thinking that engenders hysteria and panic. One million of the six million people who heard Orson Welles's broadcast of H. G. Wells's *War of the Worlds* are reported to have panicked. Many reported that when they saw others panicking, they took it as confirmation of the warnings on the radio and also became frightened. Well, God's calming assurance, "Do not be afraid," challenges us to remain independent of the judgments of other people. Note again the juxtaposition of fear and faith in this passage.

To the prophet Jeremiah, the Lord gave the following message:

"Do not say, 'I am only a child.' You must go to everyone I send you to and say whatever I command you. Do not be afraid of them, for I am with you and will rescue you," declares the Lord.[3]

Essentially, we must not be afraid of other people. Perhaps most of your fears are fears of other people. You fear people more than things. However, this Biblical command offers you a profound hope: you do not have to fear anyone. I call this a command, but it is more than a command. Although its words are couched in the imperative, it is in this case an imperative with promise. It is saying, "Do not be afraid of them; you do not have anything to fear from them." The cure-by-faith method of conquering fear applies mainly to the fear of people. Great! We do not need to fear relationships. We can maintain openness to those around us and can confidently love and be loved. The employee does not have to fear the overbearing boss, the wife does not have to fear the domineering husband, young people do not have to fear the cruel parent, blacks do not have to fear whites. Later in *Jeremiah* in a similar message, God says to the Hebrew people, "Do not be afraid of the king of Babylon, whom you now fear. Do not be afraid of him, declares the Lord, for I am with you and will save you and deliver you from his hands."[4] An abbreviated form of this message can apply to you and me, "Do not be afraid of . . . whom you now fear." How much more relevant could the promise be? If you could understand that the promise of deliverance from fear applies to those specific objects you are now afraid of, you would significantly benefit.

I have said that the command "Do not be afraid of people" offers you a profound hope. This hope is made extremely clear in another passage in *Jeremiah:* " 'So do not fear, O Jacob my servant: do not be dismayed, O Israel,' declares the Lord. 'I will surely save you out of a distant place, your descendants from the land of their exile. Jacob will again have peace and security, and *no one will make him afraid.' "*[5] The emphasis here is still upon the fear of people, and the hope offered is of ultimate delivery from the fear of anyone. It is possible for you to reach the point where no one can make you afraid. After long training by the Master, the disciples eventually progressed to that point. In the book of *Acts* they appear transformed from what they were in the Gospels. In them the promise of Jeremiah that "no one can make him afraid" was fulfilled, and it has been fulfilled in many other people since. You too can learn to overcome the intimidation of anyone.

Like Jeremiah, the apostle Paul was one who frequently heard God's encouragement, "Do not be afraid." Soon after his first arrival in Corinth, he had a vision in which Jesus said: "Do not be afraid; keep on speaking, do not be silent. For I am with you, and no one is going to attack and harm you, because I have many people in this city."[6] Perhaps, as you read this, it is becoming clear how solicitous God is of people's fears.

As a chaplain in combat I once experienced an encouragement like Paul's. In 1970 my troops, who had been fighting in South Vietnam, were required to cross into Cambodia to invade enemy supply lines. We did not know what we would face in that unfamiliar territory, and we were scared.

Although we did not encounter much resistance at first, during the night we could occasionally see headlights deep in the jungle and hear enemy trucks driving past escaping to the west. At our firebase I slept in a bunker which was little more than a hole in the ground, its top covered with sandbags level with the terrain. I was accustomed to such bunkers, but the strange thing was the location of the firebase. It occupied a clearing on the jungle floor, a broad expanse cut out by the natives for their slash-and-burn agriculture and totally surrounded by a teakwood forest. Seldom would we establish a firebase on flat terrain, preferring hills from which we could lob shells onto targets below or lower our artillery tubes for direct fire. It was rather disconcerting to bivouac on level ground without the advantage of height or good fields of observation. Furthermore my bunker was near the perimeter of the firebase in what, I feared, would be the first position overrun, should the enemy counterattack.

That night I bade good evening to the staff and lugged my rucksack toward my bunker, casting a fearful glance toward that seemingly impenetrable jungle nearby. Spreading my sleeping bag and removing my boots, I lay down to rest. I felt so alone, so cut off, so abandoned. I was on the opposite side of the planet from my home and family, sleeping in a triple-canopy jungle, so dense that sunlight never reached the floor. For just a moment, I must admit, a very vivid question passed through my mind, "Is God in Cambodia?" No sooner had the thought occurred than a warm feeling of peace passed over me, and I laughingly said to myself, "Of course, God is in Cambodia. He is everywhere." In my bunker then I bowed my head to pray and, sure enough, I sensed his reassuring presence. He was there! Perhaps in the same way God had anticipated Paul's fears in a strange city and was assuring him, "Of course, I am in Corinth."

In many ways the apostle Paul is an inspiring example of fearlessness. Much of his story is the narration of his last journey to Jerusalem, and a dramatic series of threats occurred then that would have halted the average person. En route he first stopped by Ephesus to address the Christians there in what he supposed would be his last visit with them. He said to them:

And now, compelled by the Spirit, I am going to Jerusalem, not knowing what will happen to me there. I only know that in every city the Holy Spirit warns me that prison and hardships are facing me. However, I will consider my life worth nothing to me, if only I may finish the race and complete the task the Lord has given me—the task of testifying to the gospel of God's grace.[7]

Sailing on farther, he docked at Caesarea where a prophet performed a dramatic illustration for him. Taking Paul's belt, he tied himself up and said, "This is what your enemies will do to you in Jerusalem."

But Paul exclaimed, "Why are you weeping and breaking my heart? I am ready not only to be bound, but also to die in Jerusalem for the name of the Lord Jesus."[8] Although warned repeatedly, Paul refused to change courses because of fear.

Eventually the prophecies concerning him were fulfilled and Paul was imprisoned in Jerusalem. Yet despite years of captivity, Paul never swerved from his allegiance to Christ. Finally, when he was deported to Rome, he experienced a sea storm, not unlike the one on the Galilean Sea. His reaction to that threat, however, contrasted commendably with that of the other apostles. Paul's storm lasted two tempestuous weeks, at the end of which an angel appeared to him on board ship with this familiar message, "Do not be afraid, Paul. You must stand trial before Caesar; and God has graciously given you the lives of all who sail with you."[9]

With that firm encouragement, Paul acted in such a manner as virtually to take over the ship. His calmness, clarity, and soundness of advice to the sailors dramatized the point that Christian courage is not merely idealistic, mystical, or detached from reality. Not at all! The fearlessness that faith produces means genuine courage in the most humanistic definition of the word. In this whole tumultuous series of events, you can see Paul's faith in Christ combatting and conquering his fears one by one.

We began with the first book in the Bible; we shall end with the last book, which shows how consistent the Bible is in its encouragement to fearlessness. One could almost claim that the basic objective of the book of *Revelation* was to allay fear among the early Christians. The message to the church at Smyrna epitomizes this objective:

Do not be afraid of what you are about to suffer. I tell you, the devil will put some of you in prison to test you, and you will suffer persecution for ten days. Be faithful, even to the point of death, and I will give you the crown of life.[10]

Here an ingredient of the cure-by-faith method pushes the results to the ultimate. It is saying that faith can conquer the fear of suffering, imprisonment, persecution, and even death. How could a person with courage like that ever be defeated? Hopefully you will never be called upon to experience any of these, but even if you are, you do not have to be afraid. When my own personal obedience to God's call led me into combat in Vietnam, I felt as though my faith was being tested to the ultimate—to the risk of death itself. Yet I can well remember how my faith was rewarded in miraculous rescues on numerous occasions and how I consciously thought, "If faith can conquer fear in this ultimate kind of experience, I know it will work in the conventional. When I return home, I will not allow any peacetime fears to worry me." Similarly God was saying to the Christians at Smyrna that faith can conquer your fear of *anything*.

I conclude this chapter with the Bible's supreme encouragement to fearlessness, the words of Jesus in the book of *Revelation:* "Do not be afraid. I am the First and the Last. I am the Living One; I was dead, and behold I am alive for ever and ever! And I hold the keys of death and Hades."[11] This verse was outlined in an epic sermon on "The Conquest of Fear," by Dr. George W. Truett, former pastor of the First Baptist Church, Dallas:

    I. Do Not Be Afraid of Life.

    II. Do Not Be Afraid of Death.

    III. Do Not Be Afraid of Eternity.[12]

I like that! If we do not have to fear life, death, or eternity, then there is nothing we have to fear. Christ Jesus holds the keys to all fears.

NOTES

1. *Genesis* 15:1
2. *Isaiah* 8:12, 13, 17

3. *Jeremiah* 1:7, 8
4. *Jeremiah* 42:11
5. *Jeremiah* 30:10
6. *Acts* 18:9, 10
7. *Acts* 20:22–24
8. *Acts* 21:13
9. *Acts* 27:24
10. *Revelation* 2:10
11. *Revelation* 1:17
12. George W. Truett, *Follow Thou Me* (Nashville: Broadman Press, 1932), p. 103ff

PART II

The Secret of the Process of Banishing Fear

6

The Seesaw Effect

Jesus' words "You of little faith, why are you so afraid?" can be likened to a seesaw, with faith on one end and fear on the other. When faith rises, fear falls; when fear rises, faith falls. The two are inversely proportional—i.e., faith at 100 percent means fear at 0 percent, faith at 80 percent means fear at 20 percent, faith at 40 percent means fear at 60 percent, and so forth. This is brought out by Jesus' use of the descriptions "little" concerning faith and "so" concerning fearfulness.

Significantly the only driving force on the seesaw is faith. It would be as if your partner on the seesaw has his feet gathered up onto the board and you are the only one pumping. This can be encouraging! It means that fear cannot harm faith—cannot undercut it, destroy it, damage it, or reduce it in any way. No matter how frightening a situation may be, it need not threaten your faith whatsoever. The only power fear has over faith is illuminating power. It can cast light upon faith, revealing how strong or weak it is.

The seesaw effect well portrays the way faith and fear operate in our lives. When our faith is strong, very few things can cause us to fear. I think it goes without saying that the degree of fear that we feel is a variable. Some things frighten us more than others. Even the amount of fear produced by a given event may vary from time to time. What may not be so obvious is that your faith varies from time to time too. One day your faith is up, and another day it is down. Some days you are trusting God, depending upon him, and relying upon him more than on other days. This was certainly the experience of the disciples. On the day of the storm, their faith in Christ was on the downswing. He was in the boat with them, but they put little stock in his ability to rescue them. Our faith ebbs and flows daily, grows weak or waxes strong, cools down or warms up. So whenever our faith is on the downswing, our capacity to fear is on the upswing. If a particularly frightening event comes along during our downswing, we will experience it emotionally more than other times. In fact, during the downswing of our faith, it is not even necessary for a frightening event to occur for us to feel queasy and afraid. Just some memory or negative thought can trigger fear, unrest, or emotional disturbance within us.

Fortunately, since our faith is the operative power in the fear-faith relationship, then at any moment we may consciously choose to interject faith into any blue mood and reverse our emotional downswing. Your volition or willpower comes into play. I am not saying that you can will yourself to be courageous or unfearful. You cannot, but there is one thing you can do: you can will yourself to believe in God. You can! Faith is within the bounds of your control. This must be so or else we make Jesus' plain command, "Just believe,"[1] utterly meaningless. To believe is a decision you can make, and in fact must make. You cannot get into faith in God without deciding to believe in him. You do not drift into it, slide into it, or grow into it.

When the Philippian jailer, for instance, asked Paul and Silas, "Sirs, what must I do to be saved?"[2], they did not reply, "You don't have to do anything." Personally I am a strong proponent of the doctrine that there is no physical means available whereby one can be saved—neither good works, baptism, nor church membership. Salvation is only by God's grace working through human faith. Nevertheless I would not tell anyone, "You don't have to do anything to be saved." You do have to do something. As Paul answered, "Believe in the Lord Jesus, and you will be saved." That is "something." You have to believe, and belief is a choice you make. The same principle of decision that holds true for saving faith, which is at the very beginning of the Christian experience, also holds for fear-conquering faith, which may come later in the Christian experience. Basically no difference exists between kinds or types of faith. The faith that saves is the same type that conquers fear. At the moment of fear, if you choose to believe in God, your fear will begin to subside. For this reason we can confidently say that if one does not choose to exercise faith, he or she has chosen fear over faith. This person may not choose fear consciously and say, "I have decided to be afraid," yet by failing to choose faith, such is the practical result. By this definition, myriads of people are choosing fear daily.

Classically it is not faith and fear that are cast as opposites in theology. The antonyms of faith usually include skepticism, doubt, disbelief, or incredulity. It is true that in the Bible, unbelief is often held up as the opposite of faith, and I do not intend to create a new theology or to supplant the concept of unbelief with the concept of fear. Depending upon the context, unbelief can be faith's opposite, but so can fear. For that matter, one modern author has even cast love as the opposite of fear.[3] However, to demonstrate that the polarity of faith and fear is in fact a legitimate teaching of the Bible, let us look at several scriptures.

The first one appears in *Psalms:* "When I am afraid, I will trust in you. In God, whose word I praise, in God I trust; I will not be afraid. What can mortal man do to me?"[4] This affirmation, written by King David during a time of dire circumstances, is proof that David understood the seesaw principle.

Another verse appears in *Proverbs:* "Fear of man will prove to be a snare, but whoever trusts in the Lord is kept safe."[5] Here again the seesaw effect is illustrated with a new concept, namely, that faith is the trigger that activates God's blessings upon us; the one who trusts is the one who will be kept safe. The paradox is that we must believe in truths that do not become operative until we believe in them.

Next, turn to *Isaiah:* "Surely God is my salvation; I will trust and not be afraid." To the roll of adherents to the seesaw principle is added the name of Isaiah. Add to the preceding this verse from his prophecy: " 'See, I lay a stone in Zion, a tested stone, a precious cornerstone for a sure foundation; the one who trusts will never be dismayed.' "[6]

Jeremiah also highlighted the contrast of faith and fear:

But blessed is the man who trusts in the Lord, whose *CONFI-DENCE* is in him. He will be like a tree planted by the water that sends out its roots by the stream. It does not fear when

heat comes; its leaves are always green. It has no worries in a
year of drought and never fails to bear fruit.[7]

The comparison of a person's faith to roots that reach out to tap
a stream of water is instructive of how faith can prevent fears no
matter when they may come since it is always nourished and
healthy.

Observe also Jeremiah's prophecy:

> While Jeremiah had been confined in the courtyard of the
> guard, the word of the Lord came to him: "Go and tell Ebed-
> Melech the Cushite, 'This is what the Lord Almighty, the God
> of Israel, says: I am about to fulfill my words against this city
> through disaster, not prosperity. At that time they will be ful-
> filled before your eyes. But I will rescue you on that day, de-
> clares the Lord; you will not be handed over to those you fear.
> I will save you; you will not fall by the sword but will escape
> with your life, because you *TRUST* in me, declares the
> Lord.' "[8]

Again you see the juxtaposition of faith and fear.

We have already commented upon Jesus' words to Jairus,
"Don't be afraid; just believe, and she will be saved."[9] Read also
his words to the disciples: "Do not let your hearts be troubled.
Trust in God; trust also in me."[10] It is clear from the context of
this latter verse that our Lord was dealing specifically with the
disciples' fears over his announced departure from them. That
his reference to a troubled heart referred to fear becomes clearer
later in the same chapter when he said: "Do not let your hearts
be troubled and do not be afraid."[11] It is significant that he begins
his discourse on fear by saying, "Trust in God," as though this
were the summary of all he had to say to them about the cure for
fear.

Paul's speech aboard the ship in the stormy Mediterranean,
which we have also quoted previously, alludes to the faith-fear
contrast in a way similar to the Master's words upon the stormy
Galilean Sea. Paul said, "Last night an angel of God whose I am
and whom I serve stood beside me and said, 'Do not be afraid

Paul.' " And immediately Paul affirmed, "I have faith in God . . ."[12]

Moses was described as experiencing the cure-by-faith method in the book of *Hebrews:* "By faith he left Egypt, not fearing the king's anger; he persevered because he saw him who is invisible."[13]

Again the author of *Hebrews* teaches the seesaw principle in writing: "Keep your lives free from the love of money and be content with what you have, because God has said, 'Never will I leave you; never will I forsake you.' So we say with *confidence,* 'the Lord is my helper; I will not be afraid. What can man do to me?' "[14]

Like the Biblical writers, every one of us has his own faith-fear seesaw. We will always live better if we keep our faith on the high side.

NOTES

1. *Mark* 5:36
2. *Acts* 16:30
3. Gerald G. Jampolsky, *Love Is Letting Go of Fear* (New York: Bantam Books, 1981)
4. *Psalm* 56:3, 4
5. *Proverbs* 29:25
6. *Isaiah* 12:2, 28:16
7. *Jeremiah* 17:7, 8
8. *Jeremiah* 39:15–18
9. *Luke* 8:50
10. *John* 14:1
11. *John* 14:27
12. *Acts* 27:23, 25
13. *Hebrews* 11:27
14. *Hebrews* 13:5, 6

7
Exchanging Fear for Faith

Faith thinking requires deep-seated change within an individual. It requires you to become a person of faith.

Fortunately genuine personal change is feasible. God expects people to change, and this fact alone indicates the possibility of it; it is reliable doctrine that God never expects what a person cannot deliver.

Jay E. Adams, a Christian psychologist, has clarified for us the process by which human change takes place.[1] It is the "put-off/put-on" syndrome or what he calls "dehabituation" and "rehabituation." The process is announced in *Ephesians:* "You were taught, with regard to your former way of life, to put off your old self, which is being corrupted by its deceitful desires; to be made new in the attitude of your minds; and to put on the new self, created to be like God in true righteousness and holiness."[2] Note that there are two factors in change: putting off the old self and putting on the new self. Both factors are absolutely necessary to change. The Scripture asserts that for permanent change in a life, one must both eliminate an old objectionable practice and replace it with a positive, uplifting practice. Before applying this concept to the subject of fear, let us consider several other applications of this change principle.

The text in *Ephesians* continues, "Therefore each of you must put off falsehood and speak truthfully to his neighbor, for we are all members of one body." The first application of the put-off/put-on principle requires liars to put off falsehood and subsequently to put on truthfulness. The liar is required to change, and how he is to change is indicated. First he is required to quit lying, but that alone is not enough. Effective change requires more than simply the cessation of bad behavior. Second he must start speaking truthfully. That step is as necessary to change as step one.

Indeed, if the liar starts practicing step two, it will guarantee step one. That is, if a person intentionally starts declaring the truth every time he opens his mouth, he will have conquered lying. So "put off lying and put on truth speaking."

The next verse in *Ephesians* applies the process of change to the cure for anger: " 'In your anger do not sin': Do not let the sun go down while you are still angry . . ." In other words, "Put off anger, put on the daily solution of problems." Then notice the next verse: "He who has been stealing must steal no longer, but must work, doing something useful with his own hands, that he may have something to share with those in need." That is, "Put off theft; put on hard work and sharing." Thus the rehabilitation of a criminal must entail more than curing him of theft; it must also involve instilling within him the habit of work. Other such illustrations of the principle could be provided from throughout the Bible.

Now, let us apply the put-off/put-on principle to the conquest of fear. If this is the universal method of human change, then it must be the method by which the elimination of fearfulness is effected. And we find, indeed, the application of the principle to fear to be remarkably clear.

First we are to put off fear. The first section of the book discussed this aspect at length. It highlighted God's oft-repeated encouragement to us not to be afraid. It dangled appetizingly before our minds the glamorous appeal of a fear-free life. It helped us realize the pervading destructiveness of fear in our lives and in society. It deplored the wanton wastefulness of most fears. Basically it acclaimed the golden possibility of freedom from fear. Now, however, we are examining the necessity, not just the possibility, of fearlessness: we *must* put off fear. Fear as a negative is classified with anger, lying, theft, and many other such ignoble traits designated to be put out of life. Fear is abhorrent, repulsive, reprehensible, and is a repudiation of the glorious life in Christ. It is part of the old self of corruption that must be put off in order to achieve the new self which is created like God in true righteousness and holiness.

In my busy life with the U.S. Army, I am daily reminded of the diffuse nature of fear, both in my own life and in the lives of others. All fears can be and need to be pinpointed, identified, and eradicated. May I explain to you my procedure? I am always on the lookout for the emotion of fear in my life. I frequently monitor my body to watch for the tell-tale signs of tension which are my peculiar responses to fear. The muscles in my toes and feet are the first things that tense up these days. If I am driving in heavy traffic, for example, I will occasionally discover tenseness in my feet, for which I will immediately address my fears to calm them. I observe my behavior—my voice, my posture, my nerves —for fear reactions.

A couple of weeks ago I was at the hospital attempting some frustrating negotiations in trying to register my wife for surgery. It was an occasion fraught with dread, disappointment, discouragement, and helplessness. Through it all I was attempting to practice a strong faith in order to cope with my turbulent fears. When I walked outside alone that afternoon, I was met by a mild, faintly fragrant spring breeze, and my senses responded to absorb and luxuriate in the beauty of the moment. With my thoughts so attuned to this book, I could not help but reflect gratefully upon the change that had transpired within me. Earlier in life I could not have enjoyed the beauty of the atmosphere at such a time as that and might not even have noticed it. I might guiltily have scolded myself for enjoying it while my wife was experiencing such pain. Now, however, I allowed myself the full enjoyment of it all. Was it that the pleasure of the environment was pulling me up out of my dejection? Not at all. Why, I had joy even before I walked out the door. My faith had already conquered my fears and had allowed me to continue experiencing the wonderful joy of Christ. Indeed it was my faith that allowed me to perceive and enjoy nature at such an unlikely moment.

I think it is necessary for you to release your fears if you are going to be rid of them, as strange as that may sound. I know it is unlikely that one would hold onto fear intentionally, and yet we are not very aggressive in our efforts to put fear out of our lives either. We must become aggressive about it! Faith is letting go of fear. Put off fear as you would put a sin out of your life. Fear is the opposite of faith in God and therefore is dishonoring to God. "Everything that does not come from faith is sin."[3] We need to repent of our fears, literally to "change our mind" about them. That is it! Change your mind about your fears. Many of us have felt the futility of trying to rid ourselves of fear while still holding onto our old belief systems. Quit your fear thinking. The cost of the cure of fear is the overhaul of your belief system. Most of us want to be rid of our anxiety, stress, depression, and guilt while still clinging to our old belief system. All we do is go in circles.

Pause for a moment and reflect how fear is the outgrowth of unbelief. It is the price one pays for atheism, agnosticism, or simple unbelief. If it is true that "God did not give us a spirit of timidity (fear)"[4], then where does it come from? Why, from our unbelief. Even some Christians must improve or change their belief systems if they are ever to conquer fear in their lives. So start by giving your fears over to God. He has offered to take away your fears; let him have them.

Let us assume now that you truly have put off fear. In that case you should be ready for the second step of the change formula. Now you must put on faith. One must be careful here, for it is at this point that a subtle temptation arises, the temptation to stop. One may have closely followed the prescriptions to put fear out of his life and by sheer resolve may have succeeded. But with the pain gone, he may lose interest in further instruction. Further data concerning faith may seem to him unnecessary or even offensive if he is not a Christian. I caution you, however, not to give up the pursuit, since to do so now would be to accept only a halfway solution to fear. The possibility of the eventual return of a fearful mind would be assured.

The New Testament contains the parable of a house from which an evil spirit was evicted.[5] Immediately after the eviction, the house was thoroughly swept, cleaned, and tidied up. However, it was left unoccupied. Meanwhile the original tenant was house-hunting and discovered the old rental still available. So he decided to move back in, uninvited—but not before recruiting seven housemates, all more wicked than himself. Fear is that evil spirit. Assuredly we may by human effort succeed in putting off fear. The caution, however, is that unless we fill our lives with another spirit, the spirit of fear will soon return stronger than ever before. Faith is that new spirit which needs to occupy our lives in the absence of fear. If faith is there, fear cannot return.

Indeed your faith is the only thing guaranteed to ward off fear. "If you do not stand firm in your faith, you will not stand at all."[6] Fear in your life must be replaced by belief. You must be reprogrammed. If you are already a believer, you need to exercise your faith more consistently. If you are a skeptic or even an atheist, you must become a believer, or else you will never be really free of fear. I grant you this is the back door to Christianity, but it is the one through which many people have entered—becoming Christians because of the peace Christian faith offers, not because they were convinced of the gospel. The intellectual arguments for converting may never have appealed to them; or in truth the arguments against religion might have seemed to them unanswerable. But when they got a whiff of the wonderful power and peace available to believers, they cast overboard their intellectual objections and unfurled their sails of faith. It is something you have to do if you are perpetually to enjoy the fear-free life.

In Alaska one time I was friend to an engineer who was filled with doubt. We talked often about the claims of Christianity, but he was a nuclear specialist, and his brilliant mind could not seem to think in my categories. One day in chapel, though, he heard a distinguished man testify how he had come to faith after observing a particular occurrence within his own life, an experience which he recognized as a plain manifestation of supernatural power. In a flash the engineer saw it! He remembered a similar experience in his own life, and in that awareness he suddenly had all the reason he needed to establish personal faith. The change in his life was astonishing, but it was the product of an emotional, not an intellectual, conversion. His intellectual problems were not all solved, but many of them were dissolved the moment he decided to have faith. They just no longer mattered that much. The price of becoming a believer is really not that high when you consider the benefits you gain.

It is by the two-factored process of putting off fear and putting on faith that permanent change transpires within you. By this you can victoriously overcome fear from now on.

NOTES

1. Jay E. Adams, *The Christian Counselor's Manual* (Phillipsburg, N.J.: Presbyterian and Reformed Publishing Company, 1973), pp. 176–216
2. *Ephesians* 4:22, 23
3. *Romans* 14:23
4. *2 Timothy* 1:7
5. *Matthew* 12:43
6. *Isaiah* 7:9

8

Liberation from the Ultimate Fear

Years ago in my first course in psychology, I was taught a valuable mental technique for coping with fear. I learned to stretch my fears to the ultimate. Suppose, for example, that I have forgotten an important appointment with my boss. Now I am dreading to confront him. What can I do about my fear? The answer is to consciously determine the worst thing that could happen to me. So I reply, "He could fire me." Next I reason out the worst possible consequence of his firing me. "Well, I might not be able to find another job."

I keep on reasoning like this until I reach a point where the consequence is either not so intolerable or not so probable as might have seemed at first. Would he really fire me just for missing an appointment? Could I not find another job? Would job hunting really be a cause for dread? Or could there possibly even be some advantage in finding another job? Perhaps for some reason I might conclude that changing jobs would be a blessing in disguise. In this case I end up not only reducing my fear but perhaps even looking forward to my walking papers. But I would also be well prepared emotionally for whatever other punishment he might mete out to me if he did not fire me.

Now I want to take that technique to its maximum possible conclusion.

"So what if your boss should fire you?"

"I would have to hunt for another job."

"So what?"

"I might not be able to find another job."

"So what?"

"I would not have any income to support myself with."

"So what?"

"I could not provide any food, shelter, or clothing."

"So what?"

"I might starve to death."

So we come to the ultimate fear: death. This dialectic demonstrates the fact that the fear of death is behind every other fear in our lives. It is the father of all fears. Man alone in all creation is conscious of his finiteness, aware that someday he will die. Not only are we aware of it, but innately we fear it. Sir Francis Bacon wrote, "Men fear death as children fear to go in the dark." The Bible speaks of human beings as "all their lives . . . held in slavery by their fear of death."[1] Little children fear death. I can remember how as a child the thought of my death held terror for me. Not children only, but even sophisticated adults fear death. Highly educated physicians often seem disconcerted in the presence of the phenomenon of death. Studies have shown that nurses and even doctors tend to avoid the dying patient because of their own aversion to death. Recently I visited a cancerous patient in a local hospital and noted how the hospital staff tended to avoid her room, even to the point of negligence in administering her pain medicine. They even located her on the Minimum Care Ward. Society as a whole seems to instinctively avoid reminding its participants of the experience they all have in common—death.

That the fear of death is the father of all other fears is a principle which I have personally proven by experience. I volunteered to become an Army chaplain in the midst of the Vietnam crisis, under the conviction that it was God's will for me, even though I knew I would certainly end up in combat if I did. So inevitably I received an alert one day to prepare to go to Vietnam. Having entered the Army under a conviction of God's will, I took for granted that this also was God's will for me. I spent much time in prayerful preparation, sincerely wanting to make the most of this experience, both for the performance of a meaningful ministry to others as well as for my own personal development. Although I held no illusions that God would show me favoritism, I did find myself involved in some innocuous bargaining. I prayed, "Lord, if it will be to your glory, I promise I will refrain from carrying a weapon and that I will write a book on my experiences when I return."

Chaplains, as noncombatants, are not supposed to carry weapons. I knew that; but with the particular enemy we were facing, I knew also that not to do so added significantly to the danger and risk. The North Vietnamese and Viet Cong did not recognize the noncombatant status of chaplains and treated them the same as any other soldier. I was thoroughly aware of the danger I was exposing myself to by this vow, but I saw it as an exceptional experiment in faith. Before that, I had believed heartily in faith and had taught others that anyone could trust Christ to the very ultimate in human dependence. Now I was willing to experiment personally in the doctrine which I had taught theoretically. But "ultimate" in this case meant death itself.

With hundreds of other men and women, I made the nineteen-hour flight to the unfamiliar tropical climate of Vietnam. After a night's rest at the debarkation base, I made my way over to the office of the senior chaplain in the country. Now you may not have detected any real bargaining in the vow which I related before, but I must admit that a thought like this went through my mind that morning: "Since I have shown myself willing to lay down my life for God, I'll probably be assigned to some hospital in the rear area where I can be protected from the consequences of my rash vow."

When I walked into the building, I was surprised to be ushered into the presence of a senior chaplain I had served with in Europe. He made all the chaplain assignments in Vietnam, and I knew then that God was caring for me. I fully expected to be given some safe, rear-area assignment, but that was not to be. He said to me, "Charles, we have you assigned to the 101st Airborne Division." Taking me over to a large map of the country, he pointed out a territory three hundred and fifty miles to the north where this division was operating. I had been reading in the media about the bloody engagements this unit had only recently been involved in and knew I was heading into an area of extreme combat.

Well, I did join the 101st and served in combat throughout my whole tour there. What of my vow? Somehow I did not lose faith in spite of not receiving a soft assignment. After all, in my promise to God I had not literally bargained for a soft assignment—

only that he might be glorified. I reasoned that if my being in combat would bring him the most glory, then he could protect me as well under combat conditions as he could in the rear area. Even if I were killed, I had faith to believe that my future beyond this life was secure and that God would make even my death work toward his glory. Twelve months later I left Vietnam safe, whole, and without injury.

After I returned home, I did write up my memoirs of the experience, though today they are stuffed away in my attic, unpublished. As to carrying a weapon, I kept that promise too, although in the field I was strongly urged by battle-hardened veterans to carry one and was repeatedly tempted to do so. I mention this not for self-glory, but only to show that in my mind at least the whole faith experiment was summed up and focused in my commitment to that vow.

I can affirm that the faith experiment was a total success. I proved to my complete satisfaction that God can be trusted in the ultimate. To me, "Faith is betting your life that there is a God," as a soldier wrote in a Flanders trench in 1914. Essentially my experience was an experiment in faith's ability to conquer fear (though I did not understand this doctrine at the time). I had continual fear, I must admit, but the more I experimented with faith, through prayer and risk and duty, the more the level of fear declined. I mentioned earlier my vow, "If faith can conquer fear in the ultimate, I know it will work in the conventional, and when I return to the States, I'll never again be anxious over peacetime dangers." Well, my level of fear after returning from Vietnam was significantly lower than before and has remained so. Usually people of faith who have confronted death seem to have a higher than normal degree of peace, confidence, serenity, and joy. Why? Because the fear of death is the father of all fears, and those who conquer the fear of death thereby break up the foundation of all other fears in life.

Let us return to our dialectic for a moment and add one more "so what?" to it.

"I could not provide any food, shelter, or clothing."

"So what?"

"I might starve to death."

"SO WHAT?"

This final "so what?" illustrates the process by which faith conquers the fear of death. Faith in Christ assures us that death need not be feared at all. So what if we die? It is not our end. It is a beginning. It is the entry into eternal life. How do we know this? We know it by faith. Belief in the assurance of our eternal life is one of the cardinal propositions of our faith. If we rest assured that we have life after death, then for us the stinger has been pulled out of death, and the fear of death is vanquished.

Recently an interesting experiment was performed at the New Jersey Neuropsychiatric Institute.[2] A psychiatrist gave some college students posthypnotic suggestions that for some eliminated the past, for others the present, and for still others the future. He gave others a vastly expanded past, a vastly expanded present, or a vastly expanded future. The consequences in each case were profound, but expanding the future was the most startling of all. It resulted in the removal of all fear of death and induced serenity, contemplation, and a feeling of self-fulfillment. Now observe, as a matter of fact, that the same result can be gained through faith in Christ, for a vastly expanded future is exactly what he offers us in his promise of eternal life.

Since the fear of death is the father of all fears, the assurance of eternal life takes the force out of all life's fears. Indeed the assurance of life after death is the only single remedy I know of capable of curing *ALL* fears by itself—the only one that is a panacea, a cure-all, for fear. I said before that you cannot cure fear permanently without faith. Now I will go so far as to say that you cannot cure fear without a faith that assures you eternal life. Whenever the disciples in the boat cried out, "Lord, save us! We're going to drown," their belief in eternal life seemed very dim. No wonder they were terrified.

It is not my purpose in this chapter to argue the fact of immortality. I do, however, want to prove that the Bible does offer it. When I was training to become a chaplain, I had a conversation one day with a Jewish chaplain who said that immortality is not taught in the Old Testament. We were riding together in the back of a truck with several other student chaplains when he made this claim.

I said, "What about Job's question when he said, 'If a man dies, will he live again?' "[3]

He replied, "Job was asking that question in doubt as if to say, 'If a man dies, he won't live again, will he?' "

I have thought about that rabbi's claim a great deal. After considerable research on the subject, I have come to the conclusion that he was wrong. The Old Testament does in fact teach immortality.

Take, for example, the 23rd Psalm. It ends by saying, "Surely goodness and love will follow me all the days of my life, and I will dwell in the house of the Lord forever." This psalm is rich in the subject of liberation from the fear of death. David flatly says he does not fear death: "Even though I walk through the valley of the shadow of death, I will fear no evil, for you are with me." David was free from the fear of death because he believed in life after death, and the very bedrock of his general fearlessness was his belief in eternal life.

The New Testament, as you know, is rich in assurances of eternal life. It reaches back into the Old Testament to explain that even Abraham believed in life after death: "Abraham reasoned that God could raise the dead."[4] That was the reason he was so willing to sacrifice Isaac, his son.

The emphasis of the New Testament is that some people will have eternal life and others will not. Let me rephrase that: some people have eternal life and others do not. Those who have it know they have it. They know they are bound for heaven after death. And yet anyone has the potential of gaining eternal life. God will give anyone eternal life the very moment that person repents of his sins and trusts in Jesus Christ as his personal Savior. "For God so loved the world that he gave his one and only Son that whoever believes in him shall not perish but have eternal life."[5]

Is it possible for one to know in advance that he has life after death? Several times I have spoken about the "assurance of eternal life." That is the issue. Can we gain that assurance? The answer is *yes.* Here is what the Bible says:

And this is the testimony: God has given us eternal life, and this life is in his Son. He who has the Son has life; he who does not have the Son of God does not have life. I write these things to you who believe in the name of the Son of God so that you may know that you have eternal life.[6]

Note simply that this verse uses the present tense in saying that you *have* eternal life. We should not speak only of having eternal life after we die. We have it now. We are already living eternal life. The moment we first exercised faith in Christ, we received it.

Doubts once came into my mind concerning whether I personally was saved and had eternal life. In those days I chanced upon the verse: "Everyone who calls on the name of the Lord will be saved."[7] I reflected back on a time when I thought I had done just that. Just in case I might have been mistaken, though, I decided to do it again thinking to myself, "If I did not do it before, I will certainly do it now." So I prayed, "Dear Lord Jesus, I now call upon your name. Please come into my life and become my Savior." From then on, I had complete assurance of eternal life, and my doubts have never returned.

Trust your soul's salvation to Christ Jesus, and he will give you the assurance of a "vastly expanded future."

NOTES

1. *Hebrews* 2:15
2. *Omni,* February 1984, p. 38
3. *Job* 14:14
4. *Hebrews* 11:19
5. *John* 3:16
6. *1 John* 5:11, 12, 13
7. *Romans* 10:13

9

Faith's Warning Light

A successful contractor who specialized in large shopping centers once said to me, "A secret of good business lies in turning your liabilities into assets." One way a person can turn his fears into assets is by using them as warning devices.

I drive an older model car that sometimes presents problems. The other day I was driving down the street when a red light came on suddenly on my instrument panel. It startled me. Trained by past experience, I knew I had trouble. I must react quickly, determine which indicator it is, isolate the system involved, estimate the cause, calculate the risk of driving farther, determine other options, and so forth. It turned out to be my generator indicator. I then knew I had an electrical problem, but at least I could proceed home. As I drove on down the street, the light mysteriously went out. As soon as I had the opportunity, though, I took action to correct the cause and ended up having to replace my alternator. All this because a simple light came on!

I suggest that your fear serves like an indicator light. Just as the dash light was related to the alternator, so fear is related to faith. Fear is always an indicator of faith problems. When you experience fear, it is a reliable indicator that your faith is down. Jesus so interpreted it, and in the boat on the Galilean Sea, he saw the warning light come on in the fears of his disciples, indicating a malfunction in their faith system. Just as a sensible driver would do under such circumstances, Jesus took immediate measures to correct the trouble by treating their faith. We should do the same thing. Every time fear appears within us, we should stop and deal with our faith. Just as in a car, it is cause for alarm and calls for immediate action.

To appreciate this approach, you need to recognize the variable nature of your faith. Faith oscillates, sometimes rising, sometimes falling. This fact must be acknowledged, but sometimes it is not. One time when I was attempting to assist a vibrant Christian lady with her fears and counseled that she might have weak faith, she responded, "There's nothing wrong with my faith." Truly she did exercise a deep and abiding faith in Christ, but she failed to recognize faith's relationship to her fears. Perhaps her defensiveness over faith arose from a misunderstanding of the relationship between saving faith and behavioral faith.

Saving faith is that faith we exercise upon entry into the Christian life. We are saved by faith. This, I am persuaded, is by far the more important faith to have. Indeed, saving faith is so important that one would do well to guard and defend it at all costs, as this dear lady was doing. On the other hand, behavioral faith is also very important within its own realm. It is behavioral faith that rises and falls, not saving faith. I am personally persuaded that saving faith does not vary and is a constant—never declining, never rising. It does not need to rise; I cannot conceive of one being more saved as a result of greater faith. Nor can I envision one being less saved as a result of a smaller faith. Yet behavioral faith can rise or fall, as is evidenced by Jesus' phrase, "you of little faith."

On the other hand, saving faith and behavioral faith are the same kind of faith. Both are simply the act of trusting in Jesus Christ. The Apostle Paul said of saving faith, "I know whom I have believed and am convinced that he is able to guard what I have entrusted to him for that day."[1] What Paul had "entrusted" to Christ was his soul's salvation. In behavioral faith we simply entrust other things to him—our financial support, our marriage, the safety of our children, our school performance, etc. If one has much knowledge of theology, he knows it takes a lot more effort to save a soul than it does to protect one's financial security. If we exercise faith for the greater, why not exercise it also for the smaller?

I read the story of a circus performer who stretched a tightrope over a street between two tall buildings. When a crowd gathered, he casually walked the rope across and back. Then, pointing to a wheelbarrow on the roof, he asked, "How many of you believe I can roll that wheelbarrow across?"

A few people hesitantly raised their hands. Pointing to one man who had raised his hand, the performer said, "Do you really believe I can?"

"Sure," the man shouted back.

"Then come up and get in the wheelbarrow," the performer responded.

In the same way, behavioral faith is putting our professed faith into action in our daily lives. It is daring to get into the wheelbarrow. Sometimes our fear is an indicator, a warning light, that we are not really trusting in Christ as we say we are. Jesus was pushing the wheelbarrow, but the disciples did not really believe he could get them to the other side.

Let us deal now with an altogether different, though fairly common reaction to fear. It is the attempt people make to sedate fear out of sight, which, in opposite effect puts the personality out of sight, not the fear. People are tranquilized, not fears. By chemical means we do not remove fear from ourselves; we remove ourselves from fear. Like the ostrich we hide our head in the sand and pretend we have escaped the fear.

Fear is probably the biggest single reason for the use of tranquilizers. It has been estimated that one in every four Americans is taking some form of tranquilizer in an attempt to ease anxiety. Many people drink for the relief from anxiety that alcohol brings. One counselor confessed to never having seen an alcoholic who was not basically a depressed, anxious individual.

It may have dawned upon the reader already how this discussion relates to the subject of the warning light. What is the person who sedates his fears doing but extinguishing the warning light. Suppose that on the day the indicator light flashed on at my dashboard, I took the car to a mechanic and said, "I want you to disconnect my generator indicator. That red light is bothering me." You would consider me quite foolish, would you not? Then what of the person who tranquilizes his fears without dealing with his faith, thereby treating the symptom but not the cause? We have mechanics who can fix generators, and we have faith which can cure fear. Would you not agree with me that it is always far better to remove the fear than merely to sedate it?

The warning lights in your car are your friends. It is certainly better to have them than not to have them. Interpreted in this manner, your fears can be your friends too. They are not a frightening enemy to tranquilize out of existence. Like the generator light, fear can serve to warn you when a trouble much more serious than the fear is brewing within your faith. Unbelief is your enemy, not fear.

From the tone of my writing, someone may conclude that I see human fear as some monstrous evil that I have added to the long list of spiritual iniquities and inescapable human foibles currently plaguing people. Not so, and I hasten to correct this as a gross misinterpretation of my meaning. Just the opposite. Indeed I have generally attempted to write in deep sympathy with the anxious person. I believe Jesus dealt with fearful people in kindness and sympathy. His question, "You of little faith, why are you so afraid?" was asked in sympathy, not in censoriousness, instructively not judgmentally. We may regret the light on the dash, but we do not condemn it.

Your fears can be your friends to motivate you to improve your faith. God wants you to have the highest possible faith and to trust him, depend upon him, and rely upon him wholeheartedly. He desires you to have such a faith in him that you can weather any storm in life in confidence, peace, and serenity. Your fears can be used as the indicator that your faith is not what God wants it to be so that you can do something about it. If you interpret fear like this, you can truly turn your liability into an asset.

NOTES

1. *2 Timothy* 1:12

10

Pray Your Fears

An effective prayer life is probably the most sought after of all spiritual qualities. It has filled the pages of Christian classics from the days of Christ Jesus down to the present age. People generally have a compelling desire to pray well. If they do not reach a level of personal satisfaction in praying, they will not practice it much. I suggest that faith thinking will give one a prayer life that will be personally effective and satisfying.

What is effective praying? We may answer this on two levels: the material and the emotional. On the material level, we may say an effective prayer is one that gets us what we ask for. For example, a young lady hears that her father must undergo surgery for a tumor. She prays that he will not have to go through the operation and, lo, she hears his surgery has been postponed indefinitely. Thus God has answered her prayer, and she feels very good about it.

On the emotional level, effective praying has a totally different meaning, for it relates to the effect the prayer has upon the person who is praying. Returning to the preceding illustration, let us observe the individual from an emotional standpoint. When she first hears that her father must be operated on, she becomes quite upset. She seeks some form of relief from her distress. She believes God answers prayer and can heal her father, and this she requests. At the same time, however, she is concerned about herself, for she feels she needs some form of relief from her terrible anxiety. She may not actually pray for herself, for it is her father who has the main need. As she prays, though, a powerful sensation of relief may quietly steal over her. She interprets it as the movement of the Holy Spirit upon her spirit, indicating that God has heard her prayer. Presently she rises, saying, "Everything is going to be all right. God has given me peace."

I have seen this happen countless times, and I suggest that this is the most effective kind of praying. It is the touch of God's hand upon the praying person, bringing serenity and peace to a troubled soul. It brings personal satisfaction and a sweet feeling of contentment that motivates one to return to prayer again and again.

You may ask, "Isn't praying that gets answers on the material level effective praying too?" You are right; it is. But the two kinds of effects normally go hand in hand. Usually, when God is going to answer a prayer, he makes it known to the person who is praying by giving to him or her this feeling of peace. Indeed, it is hard to believe one is praying in faith if that person does not achieve peace after having presented a request to God. On the other hand, a feeling of peace may come to a praying person even when his specific request is denied. I think this can be true because it is God's way of saying, "Everything is going to be all right—even if I do not choose to honor your specific request." The Lord, in his infinite wisdom, may choose to have the father go through the surgery while still conveying to the praying person that everything will be okay in the end. This is why I say the most effective praying is the kind that benefits the one who prays, that affects him on the emotional level.

For example, I recall that in Vietnam one particular day I experienced the unique peace of mind that comes after effective prayer. It occurred during a very busy period when I was hopping by helicopter from place to place for the purpose of conducting unit worship services. The location was along the jungle banks of the famed Perfume River, west of Hue. My unit maintained a basecamp, known as Landing Zone (LZ) Sally, in a populated area near the South China Sea coast, and I had a hard-sided tent there (though I seldom saw it). Most of the time, I was out in the jungle or at our forward staging area, Firebase Birmingham. Birmingham was situated like a citadel atop a mountain, guarding the approaches to the cities from the jungle. In addition to my tent at LZ Sally, I also claimed a residence on Birmingham, a structure engineered out of sand-filled ammunition boxes. We called it a "hooch."

On the afternoon in question, I was a passenger aboard a supply helicopter flying into Firebase Birmingham. Before we landed, I shouted to the crew chief, "Are we going back to LZ Sally?"

"We will in about an hour," he replied. "We have another mission or two to fly."

"Good," I thought to myself, "that will just give me enough time."

For several days I had hoped to find a free hour at my hooch when I could complete a tape-recorded letter to my parents, and now I saw my opportunity. When we landed, I jumped from the helicopter and hastily lugged my rucksack up a steep incline to my abode. Quickly I set up my recorder and began transcribing. Meanwhile I could hear the helicopter landing and taking off on two more sorties, but my recording was taking longer than I had anticipated. As I approached the hour's limit, I cut the recorder off, bowed my head, and prayed, "Lord, help me not to miss my ride to Sally!" It was imperative that I get back in order to conduct a service on the coast the next day.

I think you must understand my personality in order to appreciate what followed. I am a very efficient, practical-minded, methodical realist. Normally I would have jumped up and run down the hill within the hour, shirttail flying. I did not this time. Instead a strange feeling of peace and assurance came over me when I prayed, and I casually turned the recorder back on to finish my task. Of late I had been experiencing increasing evidences of God's hand upon my life, and I felt it very clearly now. It was a pleasurable feeling of confidence that God would answer my prayer.

It was nearly dusk when I completed the tape and repacked. I had not heard the helicopter for quite a while, but I felt no anxiety. About this time I looked out my window and saw the supply sergeant returning to his hooch.

"Sarge," I shouted, "is the chopper coming back?"

"No, chaplain," he replied, "he's already gone off station."

Strangely I felt no anxiety and continued to pack. I walked on out to the helipad and asked a couple of men if there would be another helicopter returning to LZ Sally this evening. By now it was tending toward sunset and one said, "Yes," the other said,

"No." I was astonished at myself as I set my rucksack onto the pad and patiently began waiting.

Amazingly a tiny helicopter buzzed down onto the landing pad and off stepped my commander. I approached him and shouted above the roar of the craft, "Sir, I need to return to Sally."

He responded, "You're lucky! This is a special bird."

I climbed into the helicopter and buckled myself comfortably in place, fixing the communication helmet over my head. After we took off, I signaled the pilot and asked him, "The ol' man said this is a special bird. What did he mean?"

He replied, "We didn't plan to fly back to B'ham today, but a few minutes ago a brigade meeting the colonel was supposed to attend was canceled for some reason. I even had another mission planned for now, but at the last minute I was taken off it to fly him out here."

I was utterly astonished! Yet I clearly knew the reason for their changed plans. God had answered my humble prayer. As a consequence, I gained a much stronger confidence in the power of prayer.

My second question is "How can a person pray effectively?" Ah, now we have asked a really old question. Remember how the apostles asked it: "Lord, teach us to pray."[1] I propose three steps:

1. Pray about what frightens you, worries you, distresses you, stresses you, or creates anxiety. In other words pray about your fears. Make your fears the subjects of your prayers. I believe this method will often solve one of the most difficult problems in praying—that is, finding something meaningful to pray about. Think about the variety of ineffective ways people pray. Some of us read our prayers, but that robs praying of the personal element. Some of us memorize prayers and repeat the same subjects over and over. Prayers that are read might even be superior to memorized prayers in that they at least express fresh ideas we may never have thought about. Some of us pray extemporaneously. But how often do we repeat the same outline, the same ideas, or even the same phrases? It is almost as if our prayers were memorized. But what good is a prayer if, after we pray it, we have failed to touch upon the subject that most needs prayer.

You see, by praying about your fears you have ready-made

subjects that are fresh, existential, emotional, and necessary—all the attributes for effective prayer. Besides, the things that cause your fear are the things you need to pray about the most. They are the things for which you need to request God's assistance. The epistle of *James* says, "You do not have, because you do not ask God."² I want to ask you to pause a second while you are reading and think about the things that are causing you fear right now. Because those are the things that are threatening you the most, they are the things in which you need God's help. They are making you feel inadequate and therefore afraid. Turn the subjects over to God. "Cast all your anxiety on him because he cares for you."³ You can ask God to change or conquer or protect you from whatever is frightening or worrying you; and because of your faith in him, he will do it.

In one place the Bible makes the procedure of praying about your fears crystal clear. "Do not be anxious about anything, but in everything, by prayer and petition, with thanksgiving, present your requests to God."⁴ It is saying, "Pray about your anxieties; request God to do something about them."

One man did just that. Have you ever read the words of the prayer of Jacob which he prayed beside the brook Jabbok, located in modern Jordan? This was the time when Jacob wrestled with God. Classically this wrestling match has been interpreted as being symbolic of praying, one of the most popular illustrations of prayer of all time. Here is a part of that prayer: " 'Save me, I pray, from the hand of my brother Esau, for I am afraid he will come and attack me, and also the mothers with their children. But you have said, "I will surely make you prosper and will make your descendants like the sand of the sea, which cannot be counted." ' "⁵ We see that he was praying his fear, saying, "I am afraid." We also see that he was practicing a traditional technique of prayer known as "pleading the promises of God." Jacob was doing truly effective praying because he was praying about his most timely issue, namely, the one he feared the most. Even so, you and I are seldom without subjects for prayer, for our fears can define our praying; and if at any time we find ourselves without fear, we certainly have high cause for another subject: thanksgiving.

2. Ask that God cure your fears. You may not at first see the difference between my first and second steps. In the first step I recommended you ask God to take away the things that make you afraid; here I am saying, "Ask God to take away the emotion of fear from within you." God can reach down inside a person when he or she is afraid and actually take away the feeling of fear. It is not absolutely necessary that the cause of our fears be removed before we become unafraid. I described at the beginning of this chapter how praying can sometimes bring to an individual a genuine feeling of peace and how prayer that achieves this is the most effective kind of praying. Well, the feeling of such peace is, simply stated, the result of God taking out of the person the feeling of fear. It is the other side of the coin. You may arrive at such peace by praying, "Lord, strengthen my faith [remember that faith conquers fear] and take away my fear."

Peace of mind arrives when fear leaves. Peace, as I have said before, is the absence of fear. If you get rid of your fears, you will experience peace in your life. There is a very interesting promise that immediately follows the instruction quoted earlier, "Do not be anxious about anything, but in everything, by prayer and petition, with thanksgiving, present your requests to God." The result of following this instruction is this: "And the peace of God, which transcends all understanding, will guard your hearts and minds in Christ Jesus."[6] Is this not an exciting discovery—that if you pray about your anxieties, God will give you peace?

An old story is told of a minister aboard a sailing ship in a terrible storm. All of the passengers were urgently praying to survive—except him. Someone asked him, "Parson, why aren't you praying?"

He replied, "I'm all prayed up."

I like that! I think he was saying that God had already taken away his anxiety and had given him peace.

3. Pray about your faith. Since it is faith that conquers fear, we must pray about our faith if we are to complete the prescription for effective prayer. The Bible gives two prayers for faith.

The first is negative. Jesus, along with Peter, James, and John, had been on the Mount of Transfiguration. When he came down, he found the other disciples surrounded by a large, contentious crowd. Upon inquiry, he discovered that a man had brought his demon-possessed son to the disciples to be healed, but for some reason they had failed. Seeing Jesus, the man said, "If you can do anything, take pity on us and help us."[7] Jesus, reflecting back the man's doubts, said, " 'If you can'?" Then Jesus added, "Everything is possible for him who believes." The man understood immediately and exclaimed, "I do believe; help me overcome my unbelief." You, too, can pray, "Help me overcome my unbelief!" Fear evidences unbelief, and unbelief is a sin. Confess it and ask for its removal.

The second prayer is positive. The apostles prayed it: "Increase our faith!"[8], which means, "Add to our faith." Since faith itself originally came to you as a gift from God, then to gain more faith just ask for it.[9]

I think a person who consistently prays about his fear and faith will experience an increase in emotional health. Many people do not do enough introspection. Consequently they often are unaware that they are afraid or of what they fear. Prayer can facilitate our analysis of moods and feelings. When you pray your fears, you must first of all analyze them, and in prayer the believer has the aid of the Holy Spirit in doing so: "We do not know what we ought to pray, but the Spirit himself intercedes for us with groans that words cannot express."[10]

So for effective praying, learn to pray your fears, which means, in summary, ask God to handle those things that make you afraid, ask God to take from you the feeling of fear, and pray for stronger faith. I once wrote a chorus that expresses my joy in praying:

> Praise God I've learned to pray,
> Unworthy though I be,
> When in despair I said to him,
> "Teach me to pray like thee."

NOTES

1. *Luke* 11:1
2. *James* 4:2

3. *1 Peter* 5:7
4. *Philippians* 4:6
5. *Genesis* 32:11, 12
6. *Philippians* 4:6, 7
7. *Mark* 9:22, 23
8. *Luke* 17:5
9. *Ephesians* 2:8
10. *Romans* 8:26

11
Take No Counsel from Fear

Dr. George W. Truett, long-time pastor of the First Baptist Church, Dallas, related a personal experience from his youth. As Financial Secretary of Baylor University, he had been challenged to raise funds to clear up a large debt. To accomplish this, he went on fund-raising tours with Dr. B. H. Carroll, an eminent pastor and president of the Board of Trustees. On one such tour the two men arrived in a Texas community where a widely publicized meeting was to be held the next day. During the night, however, a tremendous rainstorm flooded the area and spoiled the meeting. Only a few people gathered that day, but Dr. Carroll proceeded to speak to them with great fervor on the claims of Christian education. Then he announced that after the singing of a hymn, the young secretary would also speak and a collection would be taken for the university. During the singing of the hymn, Truett wrote to Dr. Carroll on a card, saying, "Because of the small company, you may agree with me that no collection should be attempted." Quickly Dr. Carroll turned the card over and wrote: "Never take counsel of your fears or appearances; do your whole duty, and you may unfearingly leave the results with God. Certainly you will ask the people to make their gifts today." Young Truett acceded to the advice, took the collection, and the results were astonishing. Women gave the rings from their fingers, men gave watches and wallets, and an outstanding offering was collected that day.

Dr. Carroll was right; we should not take counsel from our fears. You may be afraid, but do not make any decisions out of fear or be motivated by your fears. Many people are. Consider the case of the one-talented man in Jesus' famous parable.[1] A wealthy man who was going on a long trip entrusted his money to three agents to manage in his absence. The one to whom he gave five thousand dollars managed it well enough to earn five thousand more before the man returned. The one to whom he gave two thousand earned two more thousand. However, the one to whom he gave one thousand said, "Master, I knew that you are a hard man, harvesting where you have not sown and gathering where you have not scattered seed. So I was afraid and went out and hid your money in the ground. See, here is what belongs to you." Obviously he made a colossal blunder for he was utterly condemned by the master in these biting words: "You wicked, lazy servant! So you knew that I harvest where I have not sown and gather where I have not scattered seed? Well, then you should have put my money on deposit with the bankers so that when I returned I would have received it back with interest." The master showed him the error he had made in his judgment: "You say your knowledge of my toughness made you do nothing; I say that knowledge should have made you do *something!*"

What caused this error in judgment? The servant explained it when he said, "I was afraid," admitting he had taken counsel from his fears. Fear always distorts judgment! It confuses, paralyzes, mesmerizes. In the animal kingdom this quality of fear is employed in conquest. The roar of the lion panics its prey. The hiss of a snake immobilizes. Many prey defeat themselves by running pell-mell or freezing motionless. Animal safety would be enhanced if there were no fear. Athletes sometimes employ the same tactic. We all know of the famous boxer who intimidated his opponents at the weigh-ins with threatening patter. How many of his opponents were defeated through sheer fright? Physiologists tell us that fright has a way of mobilizing the body for action through the infusion of adrenaline into the system, but we also know that it often immobilizes the mind. The one-talented man would have been better off to have disregarded his fear than to have acted on it as he confessedly did.

In another illustration, fear again kept people from taking sensible action. When Jesus was on earth, there were many state leaders in Jerusalem who believed in Jesus, but "because of the Pharisees," the Bible says, "they would not confess their faith for fear they would be put out of the synagogue; for they loved praise from men more than praise from God."[2] One wonders how many more people today would become professed Christians were it not for fear. Some groups today use the Pharisees' tactics. They deliberately use intimidation to thwart the conversion of their members to Christianity. When will believers become aware that unbelievers are engaging in a game of wits, that intimidation is their favorite tool, and that we have the perfect defense against intimidation in the form of our faith if we would only use it? Yet never, never are we to seek to intimidate others in return. We are not to take up their weapons. Indeed we possess a far superior weapon—our faith! If we would only use it!

Think how often we take counsel from our fears. For example, fear frequently paralyzes a person in public speaking. Why? Because he fears the crowd; he loves their praise. A brilliant young preacher was to address a great assembly of his denomination. Taking counsel from his fears, he stopped at a bar on his way to the auditorium to get a bracer. He never made it to the pulpit. His sin was not in his alcoholism; it was in his unbelief. He was putting alcohol in the place of faith, seeking from alcohol what he should have sought from faith. Mind you, I am not saying that you should approach the speaker's stand "cold-turkey." No, approach it strongly undergirded by faith.

I can think of so many other examples of people taking counsel from fear: defensiveness, drugs, passivity. So many great worthy, God-inspired projects have been totally blocked because good people took counsel from their fears.

Turning the scene, consider an illustration of one who, like Carroll and Truett, refused to take counsel from his fears. Charles Haddon Spurgeon, in an incident in his youth, had just become a Christian when one day he was walking alone through a dark forest around dusk. Suddenly a specter seemed to loom before him. In fright he halted but did not run. Deciding to take advantage of his new faith, he resolutely walked on down the path toward the specter, only to discover it was just a shadow. He had bravely refused to take counsel from his fears and apparently learned a lifelong lesson. God takes care of you. You may be afraid, but walk bravely forward in the way you should go, totally disregarding the counsel of your fears, and you will be consistently victorious.

If we are not to take counsel from our fears, what are we to take counsel from? Why, from our faith! Fear gives you negative advice; faith gives you positive advice. Your faith often counsels you to attempt some awe-inspiring, dream-fulfilling project while in your ear fear keeps whispering, "It won't work. You will fail. They will criticize you. The risk is too great. For safety's sake, don't try it." Faith and fear compete within your very soul. The noble way, the best way, the victorious way is always to ignore fear's enervating advice and ever to follow faith's energizing advice.

NOTES

1. *Matthew* 25:14–30
2. *John* 12:42

12

"I Didn't Know I Was Afraid"

In closing this section I shall present two case studies illustrating the process by which faith conquers fear. The study in this chapter is of the life of the apostle Peter. To us, the value of Peter's life lies in its transparency. It presents us with a classic study of faith and fear. Authors have often created great drama by depicting two opposing forces vying for expression in a single life. In Peter it was a struggle between fear and faith. This struggle—and we all experience it—summarized his whole life from an emotional standpoint.

Ultimately faith won the struggle, for it was Peter who eventually penned the expression, "Cast all your anxiety on him because he cares for you."[1] These were words alive with meaning for Peter, expressing his own personal understanding of faith's conquest of fear, an understanding he had gained through years of painful experience. This sentence was written late in Peter's life, so let us go back in time to a period in which he did not understand this formula nor, for that matter, see any importance in it.

Earlier in his life Peter would not even have known he had fear; nor would anyone else. Brash, abrupt, impetuous, self-confident, he presented anything but the image of a fearful man. It is the same today: some people, with lightning-and-thunder personalities, can convince the public that they are fearless and indomitable. Yet lurking beneath the surface are fears of which they themselves are unaware. It was that way with Peter. Once, he confidently vowed to Christ, "Even if all fall away, I will not."[2] Even when Jesus predicted his denial, right after this rash statement, Peter went on to affirm, "Even if I have to die with you, I will never disown you."[3] He was not in touch with his fears. This was a far different Peter from the one who penned that formula, "Cast all your anxiety on him because he cares for you."

Unlike Peter, many people never learn to conquer fear. When they are immature, they may suppose that the older one gets, the less fearful one becomes; but this is not the case. Many people never grow out of fearfulness; and unless one particular ingredient is inserted into a life—namely, faith—a person never will absolutely conquer fear. Education will not do it. Some of our most brilliant citizens are the most frightened, since they are aware of threats that the average person scarcely suspects. Like Peter in his early days, hosts of people today are living self-defeating lives permitting a curable malady to plague them—fear.

Jesus Christ took compassion on Peter and proceeded to instruct him in how to live victoriously, with special emphasis upon the conquest of fear.

One of Peter's most important lessons was on the identification of fear in his life. It is a universally needed lesson because fear is universal. I have not singled out Peter as though he were the most fearful of the disciples. On the contrary he was probably the most courageous. He seems to have been the leader on every occasion. In every list of disciples, he was always first and was their common spokesman. Although the Bible does not say so, I believe it was Peter who awakened Christ in the boat and said to him, "Lord, save us! We're going to drown!" If even Peter was susceptible to fear, then so were they all. If Peter, then we too!

Observe some of the incidents our Lord used to help Peter get in touch with his fears. Christ used, and likely even planned, numerous events to teach his followers this great faith/fear lesson. One of the most obvious of such events was the Galilean Sea storm. If Jesus had not pointed out his fear so forcibly, Peter may never have noticed it on that occasion or may never have seen any connection between it and his faith. I can imagine Peter being utterly bewildered by Jesus' quick words, "You of little faith, why are you so afraid?" He may have thought to himself, "What's that got to do with this?" Yet the very timeliness of the remark probably caused Peter, after the storm, to give profound attention to it and to reflect upon it many times in the future. He had been afraid and he could not deny it.

Another incident of fear took place on that same sea.[4] The Master and his disciples had been ministering to a crowd by the seashore (in the incident of the feeding of the five thousand). At dusk Jesus had compelled the disciples to get into their boat and embark for the opposite shore. Dutifully they had obeyed, while Jesus dismissed the people and went up into the hills to pray. The boat encountered a strong headwind on this tumultuous sea, and the disciples had to strain hard at the oars. Interestingly one of the Gospels records that Christ "saw them."[5] He was praying—and yet he saw them. I see a twofold significance in this observation: first it was the disciples he was praying for that night, and second it symbolized how today Christ watches our lives, intercedes for us, and is ready to come to our assistance at any moment, just as he miraculously went to the aid of the apostles.

To get to them, he simply walked out on the water to the boat. Seeing him coming, they almost panicked, in response to which Jesus calmly said, "Take courage! It is I. Don't be afraid." With those words he announced to them the meaning of the event—namely, the conquest of fear. With his typical impetuosity, Peter blurted out a strange request: "Lord, if it's you, tell me to come to you on the water." Now that is enthusiasm! I do not believe that Peter's impulsive remarks on occasions such as this were all bravado or show-offishness. Considering his nature, I believe they arose out of his zealous admiration and growing love for Christ Jesus. His prayer was answered: "Come," said Jesus.

Immediately Peter climbed over the side of the boat and walked on the water. At this point a peculiar observation is recorded: "But when he saw the wind, he was afraid." The peculiarity is not that he "saw" the wind, as implausible as that may sound, for this, I believe, simply means he saw the wind acting on the water or the boat, or his own robe flapping in the breeze. No, the peculiarity is that it was the wind that made him afraid. Not the water, but the wind. Here was Peter, walking on water, a feat that would normally provoke fear (I suppose) but held none for Peter, while fearing a breeze, a phenomenon which normally provokes little fear but frightened Peter. Now that was just like Peter: he could strike out on great enterprises only to be tripped by trivialities. Why? Because he was out of touch with his fears. He needed to learn to recognize his fears.

As a consequence of his fear, Peter began sinking into the sea. Immediately Jesus reached out his hand and caught him. Again there came from Jesus' lips one of his startling remarks, "You of little faith, why did you doubt?" Here is a new point in the fear/faith lesson. His words contrast with those during the first storm, "You of little faith, why are you so afraid?" Here doubt takes the place of fear, in the polarity with faith. It is saying, "Fear is doubt." Peter was fearful only because he doubted his safety in the presence of Christ. What a swift seesaw Peter was on that day! Rapidly his faith and fear were working against each other. His faith would rise and his fear would fall; then, suddenly, his faith would fall and his fears would rise. When his faith was up, he could achieve the impossible; but when his faith fell, his victories quickly vanished.

Peter needed to be aware of his fearfulness, desperately so. An event was fast approaching in which the consequences of his fearfulness would be infinitely more serious than anything he had ever faced before. If he had not learned about his own tendency to fear before then, he would sail into that event totally unprepared, even as he had done before.

Unfortunately, when the new event rolled around, Peter still had not become aware of the depth of his deficiency of faith. As late as the evening before the crucifixion, Peter was boasting that he had the courage to follow Christ even to death. Even Christ's plain prediction that Peter would deny him before the cock crowed the next morning failed to arouse Peter to an awareness of his fear. Then Jesus led the disciples into the Garden of Gethsemane and gave them another grave warning, "Watch and pray so that you will not fall into temptation."[6] Their greatest temptation, then, was fear. Jesus was admonishing them to pray their fears, but how could they do so if they were not aware of them?

So Peter entered that Good Friday totally unprepared. He was brave in daring to enter the very courtyard of his enemy while his Master stood on trial but not brave enough. It was not the threat of the cruel high priest nor the sword of Roman soldiers that finally unnerved Peter. It was nothing deadlier than the tongue of a lowly servant girl. She simply said, "You also were with Jesus of Galilee."[7] But somehow, for Peter, in that little pink tongue focused the total force of all the threats that had ever plagued his life—the sea storm, the deadly wind, all of it. Peter's quick reply was this: "I don't know what you're talking about." His denial was as impetuous as his affirmations had been. For Peter, though, this one event was not to end the test, and the second one was like the first, equally lowly, equally devastating. Another maiden exclaimed, "This fellow was with Jesus of Nazareth," to which Peter responded with an oath, "I don't know the man!" Another hour passed before the third wave of fear was to engulf Peter, this time in the reproaches of a group of observers saying, "Surely, you are one of them for your accent gives you away." And again there came forth from Peter the denial and curses, "I don't know the man!"

Peter failed this gravest test of all, and yet even this did not mean total failure for him. Jesus simply took this event, just as he had done with the others, and turned it into a training experience for Peter, a final lesson in the identification of fear. I believe that Peter at last learned his lesson, for that event seemed to put him in touch with his fears. From then on, there would be no more weaving, bobbing, ducking, dodging, or denying his fearfulness. Now it was out in the open and plain for all to see. Peter was no better than anyone else. He too was a man of fear. Yet in learning this lesson, Peter was enabled to make that great leap out of fear into courage, serenity, and peace, for from that weekend forward, Peter was a new man. How different was the Peter of Good Friday from the one of Pentecost who stood bravely before thousands and exclaimed, "Let all Israel be assured of this: God has made this Jesus, whom you crucified, both Lord and Christ."[8]

Not the denial but the admission of fear is the first step toward fearlessness. Many of us are denying our fears. One of the biggest tasks of counselors today is the helping of people to uncover their fears—"phobias," they call them, a sophisticated name for fear. They say we repress our fears, displace them, or transfer them. In counseling, when a person outwardly complains of anxiety and tension and anxiety-related symptoms, his chances of help are usually good, but when one denies his anxiety, the path of ther-

BANISHING FEAR FROM YOUR LIFE

apy is likely to be very difficult. What is true in psychology is also true in the spiritual realm. In the cure-by-faith method, the personal identification of your fears is absolutely essential to success. The moment Peter finally recognized his fears, he took one giant step toward faith.

NOTES

1. *1 Peter* 5:7
2. *Mark* 14:29
3. *Mark* 14:31
4. *Matthew* 14:22–34; *Mark* 6:47–54; *John* 6:16–21
5. *Mark* 6:48
6. *Matthew* 26:41
7. *Mark* 14:67f
8. *Acts* 2:36

13

"It Took a Lot to Conquer My Fears"

A sweeping examination of the Bible will impress one with the large amount of content devoted to the conquest of fear. From the list in *Hebrews* 11, "The Faith Hall of Fame," for example, consider how many of those heroes of faith began in fearfulness —Abraham, Isaac, Jacob, Joseph, Moses. Their stories traced their progress from fear to abiding faith, a pilgrimage which any one of us can take.

In the Old Testament one of the clearest journeys from fear to faith was made by Gideon.[1] Gideon began as an obscure young man but grew to become a mighty general. He lived in a time of great oppression, when a multitude of desert people from the east were invading Israel during harvest times and pillaging everything the Israelites owned and produced. It was a time of great fear in Israel.

SCENE 1

Scene 1 opens with the young man, Gideon, threshing wheat clandestinely in a winepress, for fear of the enemy. In this modest setting I cannot say whether or not Gideon felt successful, but in light of what happened later, he certainly had not reached the peak of his potential. Gideon is portrayed as a person of low self-esteem. In a similar manner many people today are threshing wheat in winepresses, their personal fulfillment frustrated by fear.

A messenger appeared to him to inform him that God had selected him to deliver his nation from the Midianites. As with Moses at the burning bush, the messenger had to pursue a dialectic with Gideon to persuade him to take the risk. Gideon did not know with whom he was conversing at first, and only as the conversation progressed did he realize it was an angel of God.

Upon that discovery, he fell into a deeper fear, a new kind of fear to Gideon, the fear of the very presence of God himself. Seemingly he had never met God before, had never encountered him nor initiated any relationship with him at all. This, for him, was the beginning of religious experience, and, as is usually the case, it began with fear and trembling. "When Gideon realized that it was the angel of the Lord, he exclaimed, 'Ah, Sovereign Lord! I have seen the angel of the Lord face to face!' But the Lord said to him, 'Peace! Do not be afraid. You are not going to die.' "

Note how early it is in his experience with Gideon that God begins to address Gideon's fears, beginning with his fears of God and progressing on to his fears of the enemy. Fear was Gideon's most debilitating and limiting factor, just as it is with most of God's servants, and it needed to be removed. God's answer to Gideon's need was the gift of peace. That is exactly what Gideon needed. What is peace but the absence of fear? When Gideon was to go to battle, he would need a heart at peace to be able to fling all his power into the conflict. Here you can see God reaching his great hand down into the heart of this man and skillfully extracting from it that enervating fear. Such was the personal experience that Gideon felt at that moment—the feeling that fear had been extracted and peace inserted in its place, for he immediately proceeded to build an altar and to name that altar, "The Lord Is Peace."

SCENE 2

Scene 2 transpired that same night. God gave to Gideon his first assignment: he was to destroy his father's altar to Baal, cut down the Asherah pole, and build an altar to God. What was happening? God was performing two purposes: strengthening Gideon's faith and reducing Gideon's fears, both of which were designed to prepare him for war. His first assignment involved minimum danger, similar to Moses' first assignment to pick up a live snake. That was cause enough for fright to Gideon, though, for "he was afraid of his family and the men of the town." Nevertheless he exercised due obedience to God's command and, in spite of his fears, proceeded to destroy the altar, though waiting discreetly till night to do so. Gideon took a little counsel from his fears—not much but a little. He was beginning to grow, daring to venture forth ever so slightly from the security of his winepress. His fear was slowly shriveling in proportion to the blossoming of his faith. He had gained a little content for his faith, a little revelation from God, as he hazarded his safety in this endeavor. The revelation which God gave to him was essentially one simple promise: "I will be with you." Clinging by faith to that unseen, unproven, untried truth, he carried out his mission—and was gloriously successful.

The high degree of risk in breaking up that altar came out forcibly in what followed. The Bible described how the townspeople "investigated" the crime the next morning and, upon discovering that Gideon had done it, demanded that he must die. Gideon was saved only by the intercession of his father. The experiment had succeeded! Gideon's faith had worked! God's promise had proven worth relying upon, and after that you can see Gideon's confidence swell like that of an athlete after his first touchdown. Strengthened by his faith and armed with God's commission, he trumpeted forth a call to arms throughout the land, and 32,000 men responded. Nothing could stop this spirited young stallion now—nothing, alas, except his own fears.

SCENE 3

Fears die slowly, even as faith grows slowly. We see the novice young general pacing in his tent as hordes of Israelites rally to his call. It really had not been that long since Gideon had cowered in his winepress; grape stains still soiled his garments, and fears still plagued his confidence. All is as it was before, except for one thing: Gideon now had the key to fear. He now had faith, and it is out of faith, I believe, that Gideon proceeded with the famous fleece experiment. Note first that he prayed his fears and second that he pled the promises of God. "If you will save Israel by my hand as you have promised . . ." His prayer is tantamount to a plea to strengthen his faith in order that his faith might subdue his fears. First he asked that there might be dew on the fleece while all around was dry. It was done. Next he prayed that the fleece might be dry while dew was all around. Again it was so. Gideon had the assurance now that indeed God was with him; and his pursuit of God's call moved swiftly after that.

SCENE 4

Scene 4 continued to depict the struggle between faith and fear. God's method was first to cure fear within the leader, Gideon, before acting to deal with it among the followers. Gideon's fears were almost eliminated by now. Not so among the population. We come now to the scene where the Lord directed Gideon to trim down the motley horde that had responded to his trumpet call at the spring of "Harod" (significantly, the "spring of trembling"). The plan was twofold: first, invite any who were afraid simply to depart, and 22,000 did so. Second, from among the remainder cull out the careless ones with the drinking test. Without telling anyone about the test, Gideon gathered the 10,000 men around that well and told them they could drink from it. There are various interpretations of how the test went, but I believe the ones that were weeded out were those who dropped their weapons and incautiously proceeded to drink, while those who passed the test scooped up water with one hand, remaining alert and armed at all times. When that test was completed, only 300 men remained.

Several dramatic principles arise from this test. The first principle is that *fear guarantees failure*. The 22,000 fearful men in Gideon's army would have been a liability, not an asset, guaranteeing the failure, not the success, of their venture. Because fear is the opposite of faith, they were men without faith; and the door to God's power in their lives was closed. Since fear is unbelief, God cannot accomplish miracles through a fearful person. The feeling of fear has the tendency to contribute to the triumph of the foe it fears or to the eventuality of the incident it dreads. When Peter first feared sinking in the water, he himself guaranteed the failure of his water walk.

Those of us who work in the military know how one single emotion can dominate an entire unit of soldiers. Like an individual person, an army is a cohesive body that exhibits changing feelings and attitudes, a phenomenon that we call "the morale of the troops" or *esprit de corps.* When two thirds of the troops were so frightened as to abandon the battlefield and return home, as was so among the Israelites, that unit had a morale problem. Severe action had to be taken to remedy it, the only effective remedy being to eliminate the fear by discharging the fearful soldiers. Fear can dominate faith within an individual too, and the only remedy is to eliminate the fear. Obviously you cannot cut off the fearful part of yourself, but you can subdue it by faith.

A second principle is that *only faith in God ensures success.* All faith must be in God and in him alone. The ultimate reason for God's reduction of the army of Gideon was that the victory might be unmistakably his, not theirs. The odds of seeing success achieved by human endeavor alone must be made so impossible as to justify no other conclusion but that of divine intervention. Numerous other events in biblical as well as secular history illustrate the same principle, as for example the Battle of Britain. Sir Winston Churchill's tribute to the Royal Air Force, "Never in the field of human conflict was so much owed by so many to so few," reflects but the tip of the iceberg of God's intervention in that battle. Such events in history, perhaps, are provided periodically to remind us that God is ever our only reliable source of confidence. Faith placed in anything other than God, even if it is in oneself, is misplaced faith and is competitive with God. I do not mean to imply that I doubt the value of self-confidence. I believe in it—strongly—and strive for the strengthening of it within myself and others. I only believe in it, though, as a by-product of faith in God, not as an attitude achieved by human pursuit. Your self-confidence, if arrived at as a result of your beauty, strength, education, heritage, status, or attainment, may in fact place you in competition with God, may be opposed to faith in God, and may one day subject you to unwelcome fears. Self-faith has no ability to conquer fear.

What is true of faith in oneself is equally true of faith in others. I do not denigrate faith in others, but again I assert that the faith you place in others is the by-product of your faith in God and is not an attitude to be sought or taught apart from faith in God. I used to be somewhat suspicious and untrusting of people. Only since I have learned to conquer fear by faith have I really learned to trust my fellow man, but it is a trust in God more than a trust in human beings.

A third principle is that *faith can succeed against all odds*. An Israelite soldier among the original 32,000 might have looked across the valley at the long line of dark tents and camels of the enemy and said, "We're vastly outnumbered." Think what the 300-man remnant would have thought! Yet with great faith in God (for the 300 were men of faith, not fear), they proceeded to the task and valiantly succeeded. Gideon had seen faith succeed in a difficult task at home; now he saw it succeed in an impossible task. One of our Army units boasts the motto, "The difficult we do immediately; the impossible takes a little longer." That is a truly appropriate claim for the power of faith in God.

A fourth principle from Gideon's test of his army is this directive: *"To reduce your vulnerability, strengthen your faith."* Have you ever gone through a "confidence course"? This is a course of physical training in difficult, strenuous, frightening, and far-fetched tasks designed to acquaint individuals with innate powers beyond their own awareness. Ordinary people, such as housewives, learn rappelling, cliff climbing, rapids shooting, etc. The main purpose is not to teach new skills. When, for example, is the average person going to need to know how to rappel? Rather it is to instill within people confidence by acquainting them with the vast limits of their adaptability and capability. A person comes out of the confidence course saying, "I rappelled down a mountainside when I didn't think I could. I won't feel so vulnerable and frightened the next time a big challenge comes my way." God was putting the Israelites through a confidence course by reducing their forces. Faith, you see, is strengthened by difficult circumstances, not easy ones, by increasing the risks, not reducing them. To teach a child to swim, you must subject him to the risk of the water. "Pray not for a lighter load, pray for a stronger back," says the old adage. The real threat of something is reduced in proportion to your faith in God. Gideon seemed to have sensed more danger in destroying his father's idols, when his faith was weak, than in destroying the Midianites, when his faith was strong.

SCENE 5

Impressively the faith/fear struggle continues on into Scene 5. It took a lot to conquer Gideon's fears, and one more faith-strengthener is necessary. "If you are afraid to attack," said God, "go down to the camp with your servant Purah and listen to what they are saying." As an indication of the degree his faith had already reached, the youthful commander does just that. While sneaking around in the enemy camp that night, Gideon chances to overhear two Midianites gloomily discussing their fears of an Israelite victory. This is the very encouragement Gideon most needs. "Their *fears,"* indeed! Their fears were legitimate fears beyond a doubt, for God was against them! However, Israeli fears were illegitimate, unreasonable, and unfounded, as are the fears of any believer in Christ Jesus. I have observed on innumerable occasions that the fears of believers are wasted emotions because that which they feared never came to pass. You would think that we would eventually realize how safe we are, by observation if not by faith. Going back to his camp that night, Gideon might have said to himself, "I've been a fool. God has been trying to tell me all the time that I had nothing to fear. It's they who should fear." "The wicked man flees though no one pursues, but the righteous are as bold as a lion."[2]

SCENE 6

Scene 6, the conclusion, is the only scene that is free from fear. Faith had triumphed, and consequently the military victory was only an aftermath. The faith of Gideon guaranteed his victory, and such faith earned him a place among the heroes of faith of *Hebrews* 11.[3]

Amazingly Gideon's battle plan seemed to have come from his own ingenuity, not from divine direction. Being delivered from fear, he was free to create, to conceive, to invent. Fear blocks creativity while faith facilitates it. When one lives in the milieu of faith, he has a wide world of freedom of choice and decision. A believer is not a puppet on a string. The God in whom he believes created his intelligence, and intelligence functions at the height of its powers in the environment of faith. Though conceived by human wisdom, Gideon's plan proved to be correct because God was in it. The victory from beginning to end was God's. Someone may ask me, "A person cannot just decide for himself the right thing to do, can he? Should not we always wait for God to reveal his will for us before we act?" Well, yes, it is the ideal to await the disclosure of God's will for you. Seemingly God had guided Gideon step by step up to that point, and Gideon probably would have preferred that he continue to do so. Sometimes—indeed, in my own experience *frequently*—this is not the case. Very often I am pushed to the point of decision by circumstances with no such directive from the Lord. We all are often forced to fabricate our own plans. Admitting even this, we need have no fear though, for by faith we can believe that God will guide our minds to the best plan. We may preface our plans with this simple prayer: "Lord, lead me to do your will and not my own. Help me not to make the wrong decision. Close the door before me if I'm wrong."

Then without fear, we may plow ahead in faith. Gideon was like Dr. J. B. Tidwell of Baylor University, who wrote in his Bible, "J. B. Tidwell plus God equals enough."

NOTES

1. *Judges* 6, 7, 8
2. *Proverbs* 28:1
3. *Hebrews* 11:32

PART III

Nurturing the Agent that Banishes Fear

14

You Are Not Alone in the Boat

In the two previous sections of the book we explored, respectively, the promise of a fear-free life and the procedure by which faith conquers fear. Now I want to focus on faith itself.

First, do not be surprised if I use the word "faith" in a slightly different way from what you are used to. Stay open to some new dimensions for the word. When you exercise faith, you are performing three separate functions. You are fellowshipping, sensing, and imagining. The first function will occupy our attention in this chapter.

To have faith is to involve yourself in fellowship with Christ. This means simply that you experience the presence of Christ or of God with you. You feel his presence, imagine that he is with you at that moment, or associate familiarly with him. Communion with him is another way to think of it. Fellowship with Christ is a diamond with many facets. Let us examine several of them.

HIS REAL PRESENCE

By experiencing the presence of Christ I mean actually realizing his presence, not pretending to do so. By believing that Christ is with you, you are not fantasizing him, as a wife might do with her long absent husband. It is more the knowing of his presence than the imagining of it, for Christ Jesus truly is with you. Nor does faith have the effect of conjuring up his presence with you, as though he were present with you when you believed but absent when you did not believe. Faith does not activate his presence; it apprehends it. Christ was continually with you before you exercised faith, but when you believed, you became aware of his presence.

So the practice of faith begins with the assumption that Christ is now with you, as surely as he was with the disciples in the boat in Galilee. In this comparison lie some rich implications. It is a proper exposition of Scripture to see in many of the experiences of Christ in the New Testament patterns of how he interacts with us today. For instance, we can believe that Christ is riding out the "storms" we experience just as he did with the disciples. He is in the boat with us. In fact the incidents associated with his experience of walking on the water could well have been intended to demonstrate to the disciples that Jesus could be "with them" throughout their storms even if he were not physically in the boat. Such incidents were designed to achieve a carryover between the physical world and the spiritual world, preparing the disciples for the termination of his physical presence with them and the inauguration of his spiritual presence. The text of the latter incident even describes him as "seeing them straining at the oars."[1] At nighttime? Indeed! And from "the mountain"? Yes! It also describes how, upon seeing their plight, "he came to them." Undoubtedly the disciples' confidence gradually increased, as did their faith in the assumption that Jesus would continually be with them watching over them, even when it did not seem possible. Then, the last words he said to them before his ascension clearly said, "Surely, I will be with you always, to the very end of the age."[2] This is a promise that we can claim even as they did, for that is the kind of world we live in.

A PERSONAL RELATIONSHIP

I now turn the diamond of fellowship a trifle to the facet of personal relationship. Faith requires a personal relationship with Christ. Here is where I depart from some contemporary definitions of faith. When you have faith according to much current usage, you are not accepting a person; you are accepting a statement. Call it a creed, a proposition, a statement of faith, or whatever, it is still just the acceptance of a statement, not of a person. This definition of faith is inadequate and misleading. It is inadequate today and would have been inadequate at the time the New Testament was written, for at that time the verb for "faith" always expected a person to be its object. You exercised faith in a person; you trusted a person; you believed in someone. It was a street word, not a theological word, and was used in interpersonal relationships, such as business dealings, to define a relationship of trust between two parties. It was never used of ideas or propositions to describe a person's beliefs in some fact or truth— only of persons. When Jesus asked his disciples "Where is your faith?" they would have understood him to mean "Where is your faith *in me?*"

Missing from much modern faith is not only the concept of a personal relationship with Christ but also the practice of such a relationship. Because we fail to define faith in relational terms, we fail to practice faith in relational behavior. I suppose that the one grows out of the other. If we had a better concept, we would have better behavior; but for certain, we need plenty of improvement in both. For example, consider the case of the swearing baseball player who wanted to quit cursing but could not. Someone asked him, "Do you curse your mother?"

"No," he replied.

"Why not?" asked the friend.

"Because I love her," he said.

His friend then said, "If you loved the Lord, you wouldn't curse him either."

That simple statement led to the conversion and transformation of the player into a great Christian leader, Dr. Charlie Matthews, and it illustrates how inconsistent we can be in the practice of faith. We say that we love God, but we do not act as if we do. Perhaps even more to the point is the fact that we do not even see our inconsistent behavior as a faith problem. "Of course I believe in Christ," we say. Because we limit our understanding of faith to a belief in certain facts, we fail to see how our faith in those facts has any connection with our behavior. The real essence of faith is more a relationship than a belief, and poor behavior reveals that we do not really value our personal relationship with Christ very highly—that we do not truly love him.

THE PRIORITY OF FELLOWSHIP WITH CHRIST

Turning the jewel of fellowship one more turn, we come to the facet of priority. Faith gives priority to one's relationship with Christ. It puts it first. A faith that contains the power to conquer fear will (1.) produce fellowship with Christ and (2.) put that fellowship first. When Jesus was in Jerusalem, many of the community leaders believed in him but refused to show it publicly. They would not come out of the closet. The reason given was they were afraid of being put out of the synagogue. The Scripture adds, "They loved praise from men more than praise from God."[3] Who had priority in their lives? Certainly not Jesus! They believed in Jesus, it is true, but they had fear in their lives because they did not have a faith that put Christ ahead of all others. The Lord stated the case for priority when he said, "Seek *first* his kingdom and his righteousness, and all these things will be given to you as well."[4] Immediately afterward he added, "Therefore do not worry . . ." Christ obviously predicates our fearlessness upon giving our fellowship with himself top priority. If the conquest-by-faith formula has failed to work against your fears, you may have failed in your priorities. And yet if you will decide to put Christ first in your life now, the formula can still work for you. Only that kind of faith will conquer fear.

COMMITMENT TO CHRIST

Another facet of fellowship is commitment. To commit, in this sense, means to pledge, bind, or obligate oneself to Jesus Christ. It is both present and futuristic. We pledge ourselves to be friends to and followers of Christ. Faith has always had an element of commitment in it, and if you decide to use faith to conquer your fears, you are obligating yourself to follow Christ in the future, or else you do not have fear-conquering faith. I do not mean to sound negative when I say that faith has a hooker, but it does. The hooker is that it obligates us to Christ.

Some groups have an ethical problem about the concept of

commitment. I once talked with a young couple who were living together outside marriage. I asked, "Why don't you marry?"

"Oh," they replied, "we don't know whether we will always feel the same way about each other."

Some people shrink from commitment to Christ for the same reason: they are hesitant to predict what they will or will not do in the future. The Bible ascribes more power to human beings than that. It attributes to us pledge power and affirms our ability to bind ourselves to a given future behavior. For example, the Gospels describe how Jesus often tried to persuade people to pledge themselves or to make resolutions. "Can you drink the cup I drink or be baptized with the baptism I am baptized with?" he inquired. "You do not want to leave too, do you?" "Simon, son of John, do you truly love me more than these?"[5] By these solicitations Jesus was seeking commitments to sacrifice, fidelity, and love. We do have the ability to commit ourselves, and the exercise of this ability is a necessary element of our faith.

HUMAN WILL POWER

So I turn the jewel of fellowship next to the facet of willpower. I have said before that faith is a decision, an act of the will. You decide to trust; you will to have faith. I do not want to overstate the power of the human will, so I must acknowledge that the power of our wills is very limited. Indeed it is virtually limited to the power to believe. Yes, we do have pledge power, but only when we are pledging ourselves to faith in Christ. To illustrate, have you ever tried to break a bad habit, to start a good habit, or in any way to seriously reform your behavior? Most of us find it to be well nigh an impossibility. Nevertheless we go on trying, sometimes for a lifetime and to little effect. Some discover their weakness of will early in life. The man and woman who told me they could not know what they might choose in their future were in their early twenties. Others keep exercising their volitional muscles far longer in life before gradually realizing they cannot change themselves. I know of a retired general who finally quit smoking in his sixties and was so surprised at his success that he gave his heart to God. He realized that such willpower had not originated in himself; it must have come from God.

A careful reading of the Bible will disclose a constant focus on the weakness of the human will. What is Jewish history except a proof of the inadequacy of human commitment? I often assert that Jewish history was God's thousand-year demonstration of man's inability to save himself. And although Jesus frequently solicited people to make resolutions, the result 100 percent of the time was a breaking of the resolutions, as though he were trying to prove to people the inadequacy of their human wills. You can see the point at which some of them—Peter and Paul, for example—suddenly realized the inadequacy of their own efforts and committed themselves merely to simple faith in Christ. They could not do it, but Christ could do it in them, so they turned it all over to him. I believe in the somewhat dated theology that God demands of us the impossible, and then gives to us what he demands, that we may give it back to him. God gives us the faith he demands of us! Still, you must believe, and faith is impossible apart from your willpower. Just turn the key of your will in the lock of faith, and you can open the power of God.

ESTEEMING CHRIST

The final facet of fellowship is esteem. Faith will hold Christ Jesus in proper esteem, appreciating his person, his importance, and his power. This is precisely what the disciples neglected in the boat. It is obvious from their behavior and dialogue that they failed to appreciate who was in the boat with them. Their treatment of the Master seems impudent to us—the way they rudely awakened him and scolded him. They probably did not intend any disrespect; but in their panicky effort to save their lives, they were irritated by his idleness. They wanted him to help bail water. "They didn't know who he was," as the Christmas carol goes.

Then, when Jesus stood up and casually calmed the wind and the waves, their astonishment also revealed how ignorant they were of his power. The weakness of their faith was betrayed by their question, "What kind of man is this?" Their faith in Christ grew visibly through this event, but it is clear that during the storm itself they had not realized who was in the boat with them.

To experience the right kind of faith, you must appreciate what Christ Jesus can do and will do. The disciples in the boat failed to appreciate what he could do. A fear-conquering faith believes that Christ has all power in heaven and on earth. It also believes in his willingness to exercise his great power for our good. The great principle that justifies our faith in God's willingness to help us is his magnificent love for us. With his great love for us guiding his great power in our behalf, we literally have nothing to fear.

In summary, the type of faith that conquers fear is the type in which the individual remains in constant fellowship with Jesus Christ. Since Christ is real, we can and we must experience fellowship with him and we must practice his presence in our lives. Actually, for such fellowship to be effective for us, it must have priority over everything else in our lives. We must bind ourselves to Christ by a decisive act of commitment. Finally our faith must be big enough to encompass Christ's magnificent power and love.

Only relational faith like this has the power to conquer our fears and calm our anxieties. That is why those two words of encouragement which we surveyed in Chapter 5, "Fear not," are so frequently coupled with the promise from God, "for I am with you."

I vividly recall an experience in Vietnam in which God's presence had a wonderfully calming effect upon my fears. Generally speaking, I was acutely conscious all through my tour there of the degree of overall peace that faith was producing in me. I observed, for example, that I was by faith able to detach myself frequently from the horror of the fighting to feast on the pristine beauty of that country, its wide, clean, unspoiled beaches surpassing any shores I had ever seen. This experience occurred within sight of that coastline.

The troops of my battalion had the mission of clearing the enemy from Hill 474, a broad mountain along the front slopes of the Central Highlands. Enemy troops had long resided in the natural caves fronting on the seaward slope, using them as a base for terrorizing the populated coastal areas. The unit in which I served spent weeks combing the mountainside in company-sized formations, striking the enemy with everything it had. In our constant searching, our silhouettes offered prime targets to the well-concealed enemy, and we suffered numerous casualties from the siege. Every day I flew by helicopter back and forth across the face of the mountain visiting my troops regularly, bedding down nightly in the field, ministering intensively to their needs, and conducting services for small bands of men. Everytime I paused for C-rations, the 23rd Psalm came to mind, "You prepare a table before me in the presence of my enemies." Those were frightening, unnerving days.

My memory of that era centers on a particular evening I spent in the field. As was my custom, I carried my bedroll with me and bedded down wherever I was at the end of the day. On this particular evening we occupied a small, barren knoll at the base of the hill with the dark rocky mountain looming ominously above us. In the early darkness we had a ringside seat to a gigantic fireworks show, as gunships guided by powerful airborne searchlights blasted the mountain with relentless intensity. After that, everything grew quiet and remained so for the balance of the night. Sometime in the middle of the night, though, I woke up and lay passively on my inflated mattress, meditating. All was still and quiet save for the occasional "commo-checks" made by a nearby radioman. As I lay there I lightly experienced the gentle, warming presence of Christ. I heard no voice, saw no vision, but I felt the clear, unmistakable presence of the Lord at the depth of my being. Lying on my back with the ocean coast several miles to my left and the silhouette of the mountain to my right, I drank in the beauty and joy of the moment. I felt real joy, in spite of the danger and loneliness of the hour. You know how someone pinpoints a moment of time and says to himself, "This is a significant moment I am going to engrave indelibly in my memory." For me it was one of those moments. Gazing at the rare sight of the unobstructed and glittering stars overhead, I experienced utter calmness, serenity, and repose. The Lord God was with me in actuality, and by my faith in him I experienced his presence and enjoyed wonderful fellowship with him. For a few moments I was completely released from all fear, tension, and anxiety, a most welcome respite in the midst of such severe danger. Faith really works! All praise to the Father above.

NOTES

1. *Mark* 6:48
2. *Matthew* 28:20
3. *John* 12:42
4. *Matthew* 6:33
5. *Mark* 10:38; *John* 6:67, 21:15

15

Faith Like a Little Child

We come now to the second function of faith, namely, sensing. To sense is defined as "to be or become conscious of."[1] Although it usually applies to knowledge acquired by the "sense" organs, I am using it to apply to consciousness acquired by any means whatsoever. Essentially I mean consciousness of the presence of God. Faith is sensing the presence of God.

Faith is akin to a very real and ordinary function that all of us experience—sensing the presence of another person in our midst. The ability to sense the presence of another person with us, even without the seeming use of the five senses, is almost universal. Most of us have had times, while sitting quietly, when we sensed something happening and have looked up to see someone staring at us. Or, thinking we were alone, we have suddenly sensed another presence and have searched and found someone in the house with us. It is to this very human ability that I appeal as one of the functions of faith.

Faith is the ability to sense God's presence. In the previous chapter, we said that the presence of God with us is a given, but that for us to experience his presence we must apprehend it. Our sensing ability is the one we use to apprehend his presence.

While you are reading just now, try a little experiment. Pause for a moment and try to sense the presence of God with you. "How will I recognize his presence?" someone may ask. Why, you sense it in the quiet, natural way you sensed the person looking at you. This is not mysticism; it is reality. To sense his presence does not require a supernatural occasion such as a vision, voice, or apparition. I am not adverse to visions, although I have never had one; and yet I have sensed the presence of God with me times without number.

When I am witnessing to someone who has never met Christ, I

attempt early on to get the person to begin sensing God's presence personally. I say something like this: "God is everywhere. He is even in this room with us right now. He is observing everything we say and even knows what we are thinking. God loves you very much." Or in the early part of worship services, I try to lead people to sense God through the call to worship or the invocation.

Between ordinary sensing and faith sensing, however, there is this major distinction: faith always involves intuitiveness. Intuitiveness in this case is the ability to sense another person with a bare minimum of evidence. For example, we may feel the companionship of someone even though that person is quietly occupying another room in the house at the time. At home I spend a lot of time in my upstairs study, but I can still sense my wife's presence downstairs. Last week she was out of town and the whole house felt different—large and empty. We have known of people who have continued to feel the companionship of a loved one while that person lingered for years in a coma. When the loved one finally died, these individuals experienced grief as though they had been experiencing fellowship with their companion during all the intervening time. There are examples of sensing even more mysterious than the above. A companion may leave home without the knowledge of the partner, and the partner may continue to sense his presence as though he were still there, not growing lonely until after discovering his departure. Catherine Marshall describes how even after her husband, Peter Marshall, died, she continued to hold her hand out into the space between their twin beds at night to grasp his hand, as they had done so many nights before, and how the experience continued to give her a sense of his presence. Our experience of God may be more intuitive than any of these examples, but it employs the same human abilities that we use in these common experiences.

Faith not only involves intuitiveness, it necessitates it. If intuitiveness is missing, then it is not faith. "Now faith is being sure of what we hope for and certain of *what we do not see.*"[2] If we get hung up on the sparseness of evidence and reserve judgment until more facts are in, we are refusing to exercise faith. I think we all have a tendency to try to remove uncertainty; but if we succeed in doing so, we have also removed faith. Faith needs the mysterious—requires it. "We live by faith, not by sight."[3] If because of an objection to the element of intuitiveness, we refuse to exercise faith, we sacrifice some valuable advantages unique to faith. Only faith can remove fear, not sight. In the boat the disciples' sight afforded them only a horrendous storm with impending death, while if they would have had faith, it would have borne its intuitive evidence of security and fearlessness.

However slim the evidence of God's presence may be, whenever we sense him by faith, his presence seems unmistakably and indescribably real to us. We may say that the evidence for his presence follows our exercise of faith. If evidence was inadequate before we had faith, it certainly becomes adequate when we exercise faith. By faith we experience God's companionship as an overwhelming reality.

I have personally observed how the companionship of God can become so vivid as to compensate for the lack of companionship of a loved one. What a great hope this can offer to singles, widows, widowers, and divorcees! My own father passed away a few years ago, leaving my mother in her sixty-ninth year. Both of them had been exemplary Christians, but the loneliness was still a crucial test for my mother. I once said to her, "Mother, I have the belief that when one loses a mate, it is possible for the surviving mate to draw so close to the Lord Jesus that the Lord's companionship takes the place of the absent mate. Have you experienced this?"

"Oh, yes," she replied, "I don't know what I would do without him."

On the other hand, I received word one day that another widow I knew was fretting hopelessly over her loneliness. With deep compassion for the dear lady, I went to see her at the store where she worked. I made the same statement to her that I had made to my mother.

Complacently she replied, "But I believe in Christ." With that curt response she seemed to reject my observation as making no sense to her. She already believed in Jesus but saw no relationship between her religious faith and the reality of her loneliness.

The faith of the former was a living trust in God; the faith of the latter a lifeless assertion. Only a dynamic, sensing faith in God can conquer anxiety; and whenever one will put her trust in God, she releases within herself bountiful provisions for meeting life's most desperate needs.

The thrust of this chapter is that faith is natural, common, human, and available to all. God has not selected a difficult, complicated, or demanding function as the endeavor that unlocks his power. Indeed it is absurdly easy and familiar to us all. The Bible even boasts of its commonality: " 'The word is near you; it is in your mouth and in your heart,' that is, the word of faith we are proclaiming."[4] Faith, both as the means of salvation and as the means of fearlessness, does seem a remarkably easy condition to fulfill, and the ease of it accounts for much of the resistance to it. It seems too easy. Our intellects are insulted. Our pride is abased. Ah! There it is, "our pride." Maybe that is why God chose the function of faith: to deflate our pride. For how can pride stand in the company of the Almighty God?

Why, faith is so commonplace to mankind that even our young offspring know how to practice it. Let me illustrate what I mean.

A little child is left at home with a babysitter while the parents go out for the evening. The babysitter, following the instructions of the parents, puts the child to bed at the proper time, turns out the light, and shuts the door. The child, however, with a little anxiety remains awake, lying quietly in his bed until his parents return home. The child eventually hears the front door open, followed by a few muffled words and a closing of the door. Sensing that his parents are home, he turns over and goes to sleep.

This is a simple example of faith, a faith that conquered fear. At some time in your life you too have experienced something like this. You may even be able to remember it or at least to recall the sensation of trust and peace you had in your childhood. This is what faith can mean for you today too, for this is the Biblical meaning of faith. It is not inappropriate to say that only a child-like faith can conquer fear. Jesus said, "I tell you the truth, anyone who will not receive the kingdom of God like a little child will never enter it."[5] That explains faith's humiliation, but it also explains its accessibility to us.

Would it not be appealing to know again the same blind sense of security you once knew as a child in your father's home? My notion of the conquest of fear is that faith can provide a feeling of security similar to that which we knew as children. The Bible assures us, "We know . . . that . . . the one who was born of God keeps him safe, and the evil one does not touch him."[6]

In combat one day I landed with the "log bird," the logistical helicopter, in an abandoned crop field nestled in a narrow valley between two low hills. The valley was like a football field, about the same dimensions with bleacherlike hills on either side and hedgerows at both ends. I walked among the men of the platoon on the "playing field" as they read their mail and loaded provisions into their gear. Suddenly automatic gunfire broke out, and all of us dove for the sidelines. I went sprawling into a natural depression at one corner of the field, fully expecting an enemy company to sweep down from that hill and overrun our position. Momentarily scattered as we were, no one near me knew what was happening. Actually I could see only one other man, and he was occupying the same hole as I. He had no targets to fire upon and lay poised with steely-eyed alertness. When the chattering noise of the weapons subsided, the youth turned toward me and whispered, "God is with us, isn't he?"

"Yes," I whispered, "God is with us." And he was too! We both sensed his presence.

Soon the fighting ceased and darkness enveloped us. I lay down out on that same field for a peaceful night's rest.

No matter how severe might be the danger we face, we can banish fear by pausing to realize that Christ is in the boat with us.

NOTES

1. *Webster's New Collegiate Dictionary,* (Springfield, Mass.: G. C. Merriam, 1979), p. 1047
2. *Hebrews* 11:1
3. *2 Corinthians* 5:7
4. *Romans* 10:8
5. *Mark* 10:15
6. *1 John* 5:18

16
Imagination and Faith

The third function of faith is imagining. Imagination must always be a part of faith, imagination being defined as "the act or power of forming a mental picture of something not present to the senses or never being wholly perceived in reality."[1] Unless you make use of your imagination when you exercise faith, your faith will be weak and ineffective. You need a strong imagination and you need to use it. Let me illustrate.

In my faith experiment in Vietnam, I started studying about angels. It might have begun as a result of rumors I heard of a Christian village that had been miraculously protected by angels. The local Viet Cong had decided to make an example of the defenseless village and to destroy it by night. However, when they tried to attack, they found the village completely surrounded by large shining figures armed with swords. The Viet Cong fled in terror. This story was making the rounds while I was over there.

Or perhaps it was my reading of the 91st Psalm. That psalm, which meant so much to me with its soldierly promises, says, "For he will command his angels concerning you to guard you in all your ways."[2]

Anyway, instead of doing an academic study of the subject, I personalized it by imagining what those truths could mean to me —what the angel supposedly assigned to me might be thinking and feeling. I laughed to myself, "Has he got a tough assignment watching after me! He has to work overtime!" and I derived considerable comfort from visualizing his presence with me. It meant I was not alone.

Then one day I chanced to find this sentence in the Living Bible, "The Commander of the heavenly armies is here among us! He, the God of Jacob, has come to rescue us!"[3] Knowing that most translations render this as "The Lord of hosts is with us," I was fascinated to read this rendition. It appealed to my judgment for I knew that "Lord" can mean "Master" and so, presumably, "Commander"; and "hosts" applies to the angels as an army. Being a soldier, my imagination was set aflame to think that I was being accompanied not only by the lower officers and troops of the heavenly army, but by the Commanding General himself. At the time we were deep within Cambodia, surrounded by the enemy and in grave danger. My battalion, although an airmobile, reactionary task force of the 101st Airborne Division, was serving as vanguard to the 4th Infantry Division in this cross-border incursion. Our own Commanding General was hundreds of miles away. In a jungle worship service I said, "Imagine how secure you would feel if our Commanding General were to visit us here and walk among us and take charge of the unit. In the same way the Supreme Commander of the heavenly forces himself is now in our midst." We were deeply comforted by this thought. Several years later I incorporated it into a hymn I composed:

> Sacred the place where God appears,
> Lord of our land, sublime,
> In burning bush, on battlefield,
> In cold or temperate clime.
> Supreme, he commands angelic bands
> Yet comes as Master where men gather.
> Hallelujah, Lord of the hosts,
> Visit us in this place.

Significantly it had been my imagining of angels that helped me gain a new insight into the marvel of the presence of God. This is what I mean by imagination being a part of faith.

I shall pose three questions on the subject: How does imagination combat fear? What are we to imagine? How can one build his or her imagination?

In answer to the first question, imagination combats fear by being the active ingredient of faith in its fight against fear. So important is imagination to faith that it must be exercised deliberately and intentionally. To appreciate the significance of this, observe what happens to us whenever we become frightened. Initially our field of awareness narrows. For example, if you were awakened by the sounds of an intruder in your home, immediately all your attention would focus upon that person. Your eyes, your ears, your reason would all dash to him like iron to a magnet. Furthermore the incident would tend to dominate your imagination. Unless you had an extremely well-disciplined mind, you probably would not think about angels or mighty fortresses or anything like that. When the storm hit, the disciples in the boat did not remember that the power that had turned water into wine was accompanying them in that boat. My point is, they should have. Their minds ought to have been well-disciplined at all times to recall the mighty power at their support. So should ours. When the going gets tough, our imaginations should be kept supple enough to revert automatically to spiritual resources.

Imagination combats fear by keeping us in touch with reality. You know how an audience reacts to a play. It may know facts about the situation the character on the stage does not know. When he grows alarmed, you think to yourself, "If he knew the full reality of the situation, he would not be so fearful." In the same way faith keeps us in touch with the unseen realities of a situation.

Psychologists use an ordinary term to describe the way a person perceives his situation. They call it "seeing." They say all misbehavior lies in faulty seeing, that is, the inability to see the objective world accurately. Poor emotional adaptation, such as inner conflicts, subjective fantasies, or wishful thinking, colors the way a person sees his or her world. From the Christian standpoint, what faith adds to a person is the ability to see a part of reality not readily available to the five senses. The way the Bible defines faith supports this: "Now faith is being sure of what we hope for and certain of what we do not see."[4] In this regard I like the way the King James Version describes Moses: "By faith he forsook Egypt, not fearing the wrath of the king: for he endured, as *seeing* him who is invisible."[5] Faith is the imagination by which we see spiritual resources, and such resources are definitely part of reality. If we fail to *see* them, we have faulty seeing. On the other hand faith helps us to track the actions and movements of the spiritual world, which exists parallel to and concurrent with our physical world. Recently I saw a Civil War photograph of a professor on a battlefield doing surveillance from a balloon tethered to the ground. In the same way, our faith enables us to peer over the horizon to view the tremendous army of God poised for our defense.

Imagination combats fear only when it is kept strong and vigorous. Just as an effective deterrent to war is a well-prepared defense, the best deterrent to fear is a well-rehearsed imagination. You must exercise your imagination on spiritual things even when you do not need them. If you wait until you are in trouble before you start forming mental pictures of God, it is too late. I have noticed the way imagination works in soldiers overseas. Some of them keep their imaginations tuned upon their wives back home almost constantly. They write letters, read mail, talk about their wives, etc. Others are weak in imagination. These seldom write to or talk about their wives. Instead they read stories and admire photographs of other women. In Vietnam one man said to me, "I can't even get a picture in my mind of what my wife looks like." Men with underworked imaginations! They are usually the ones who are unfaithful to their wives. Spiritual thinking works very similarly to this. The wife is separated from her husband by an ocean, just as God is separated from us by a physical gulf. The husband must think often about his wife for her to remain real to him, and we must think often about God that he might remain real to us also. If a husband does not imagine his wife often, he will be tempted to have another fill her place. If we do not imagine God often, something else will begin to fill his place too.

I do not believe anyone is inherently weak in imagination, although one's imagination can suffer through neglect. Imagination, like muscles, can atrophy (is this not one of the results of TV abuse?) Therefore we all need to polish up our spiritual imaginations. Let them soar! Envision spiritual truths! Form mental pictures of God's promises as they apply to you personally.

The second question is "What are we to imagine, if imagination is to be a part of faith?" The answer is "A person and possibilities."

In our faith we are to imagine a person—the person of Jesus Christ. Just as a husband sets his imagination on his wife back home, even so we are to set our imagination on Jesus. When you are afraid, think about him; imagine that he is with you. When you do that, you are beginning to exercise faith.

Listen to the observations of the obscure prophet Zephaniah: "The Lord, the king of Israel, is with you; never again will you fear any harm."⁶ Marvelous! He says that when we become aware that the Lord is with us, we will not be afraid. Do you find it hard to imagine God? I certainly do. Always have. Fortunately we do not have to try to imagine him *per se*. We are given thousands of word pictures of God with which to form our mental pictures. Zephaniah goes on to say, "On that day they will say to Jerusalem, 'Do not fear, O Zion; do not let your hands hang limp. The Lord your God is with you; he is mighty to save. He will take great delight in you.' " You might not be able to imagine his face, but you can imagine him being happy over you. " 'He will quiet you with his love.' " If you imagine yourself growing very serene, you have a mental picture of God and his love. " 'He will rejoice over you with singing.' " You can just imagine God singing the "Hallelujah Chorus" over you. However you may do it, imagine the presence of God with you.

Second imagine possibilities. Faith not only imagines the person of God, it also imagines some good thing that is going to happen to you. To conquer fear, just imagine that God is about to do something good for you. Someone may say, "That sounds like Pollyanna thinking to me." Not so! There is this difference: We are *guided* in what good thing to imagine and do not need to fantasize, dream, or conjure up a hypothetical situation. We are to sharpen our imagination on the promises of God. You have heard the concept of "pleading the promises of God," have you not? Basically that is what I am referring to. Whenever you are afraid, think of a promise of God and imagine that promise being fulfilled for you.

Indeed, you do not even have to think of a specific promise to have something to imagine. You can just think of some commonplace Biblical description of God and derive an implied promise from that. There is a clear example of an implied promise in the apostles' experience on the stormy sea. I think they must not have heard what Jesus said to them when they got into the boat: "Let's go over to the other side of the lake."[7] Why, they already had absolute assurance of safety, because obviously they were not going to perish in the storm. No, they were going to get to "the other side." Jesus knew they had very little faith in him because they did not believe his word.

Another example of faith in an implied promise came from Abraham[8]: "By faith Abraham, when God tested him, offered Isaac as a sacrifice. He who had received the promises was about to sacrifice his one and only son, even though God had said to him, 'It is through Isaac that your offspring will be reckoned.' Abraham reasoned that God could raise the dead . . ." Abraham "reasoned" (deductive reasoning) like this: "God has promised me descendants through my son Isaac. Now he wants me to sacrifice him. Therefore he plans to raise him from the dead." Thus Abraham had "faith," such faith as even to assure him that Isaac would survive the ordeal. That is what he implied when he told his servant at the foot of the mountain: "Stay here with the donkey while I and the boy go over there. We will worship, and then *we will come back* to you."[9]

Abraham had set his mind to work upon an apparent contradiction by God—the promise of descendants through Isaac and yet the order to slay Isaac. He speculated that God perhaps would perform a very farfetched act: he would resurrect Isaac from the dead after Abraham had slain him. Armed with the mental picture of God resurrecting Isaac, he raised the knife. Resurrection happened not to be God's plan, but the fact that God used another plan to reconcile his own integrity did not bother Abraham. Abraham's ultimate faith was not in his own speculation but in the veracity and love of God. Nevertheless you can see how Abraham used his imagination to undergird his faith.

It would be possible to give dozens of other Biblical illustrations of imagination at work in faith, but let me give a contemporary one, instead. Corrie Ten Boom in her book, *Tramp for the Lord*, told how she and her sister Betsie in the concentration camp were discussing a vision Betsie had seen. It was of the two of them traveling the whole world taking the gospel to all.

"To *all* the world," objected Corrie. "But that will take much money."

"Yes, but God will provide," Betsie said. "After all, he owns the cattle on a thousand hills. If we need money, we will just ask the Father to sell a few cows."[10] I chuckled to read that. Betsie Ten Boom just set her imagination to work upon a simple biblical concept and unearthed an implied possibility and promise.

I said in a previous chapter that the word *faith* always expects a person to be its object. How then can I say a promise can be its object? Simple! A promise is a person's word, and when you believe in a person's word, you believe in that person. To doubt his word is to doubt his person. Christians believe the Bible to be the word of God; therefore when you believe in God's word, you believe in God and vice versa.

So, believe in a promise and imagine its possibility in your life and you have the makings of genuine faith.

The third question is, "How can one build his or her imagination?" Essentially your imagination needs something to feed upon. Imagination does not usually work in a void, forming mental pictures out of its own creativity. It requires something objective on which to sketch its pictures.

I saw imagination at work during the Christmas season in Vietnam as I watched a young soldier. I had flown into his location on a "log bird" filled with Christmas cards and packages. It was inspiring to watch the men reading letters and sharing cake and cookies with one another. The man I noted in particular was a tall heavy-set man solitarily engaged in opening a large box. Carefully removing the packing, he uncovered a small commercial Christmas tree. Very tenderly he lifted the tree from its box and set it up on the ground. Then, rising to his massive height and unconsciously clasping his hands in front of him, he proceeded to gaze down at that tree for an extended period of time. It was a sight to behold. Out on a treeless hilltop in Vietnam, completely lost to his own thoughts amidst a squadron of GIs, a gigantic young man bowing reverently before a minuscule bauble, framing fantasies of far away. For a few minutes he was a child back home again gathered with his family before their yuletide tree. Such is the awesome power of imagination!

The soldier was cultivating his imagination upon a material object, for that is how imagination germinates. Earlier I discussed how men overseas either grow closer or farther away from their wives when separated, depending upon how well they visualized their wives. What is it that stimulates their imaginations? Why, the flow of correspondence from back home. Like the soldier with the Christmas tree, men's imaginations feed upon material objects. During the time I was in combat, my wife Martha and I kept a voluminous flow of correspondence moving between Vietnam and the States—letters, tapes, packages. I found my imagination activated as equally well by my own correspondence as by hers. Whether I was reading her mail or writing to her, I always felt her presence with me at the time. I saw her before me, imagined the apartment as she described it—the children, the car, the pet. I stood under the old tree and wept with Dan and Lisa as Martha described the funeral of "Hamsty," their little pet hamster. I stood beside her by the old Mustang and fretted over the stolen radio antenna. I sat in the congregation with her at church and thrilled to hear the cantata. Could I have spent so many hours visualizing the presence of my wife apart from that correspondence? Not at all. It was essential to my imagination.

In the same way, one's imagination of the person and promises of God is equally dependent upon material objects. Fortunately we have plenty of such objects at our disposal—the Scriptures! The Bible is the paramount stimulant to our imagination of God. It was written imaginatively by men with vivid imaginations. The Hebrew language is a picture language, and so is Greek to a great extent. We need to learn to read the Bible imaginatively as did Betsie Ten Boom. If we can read it and not visualize it, the reason may be because we do not believe it—our faith is weak. If I could read my family's correspondence and fail to visualize their presence, it could only be because I did not care for them. Do we believe in and care for God, or not? Do we trust his word? The strength of our imagination of him will reveal the answer. Strengthen your faith by strengthening your imagination.

The way to imagine the Scriptures is to portray in your mind's eye what it says as you read it. Mull it over. Meditate upon it (for this is the real secret to meditation). Draw out its ramifications and apply them to your own life. Use deductive logic upon it. The apostles should have deduced from Jesus' earlier statement that they were not going to drown. We too, for example, can deduce that because "whosoever believes in him shall not perish but have eternal life," we then have eternal life. If we have eternal life, then we shall never die. Stand before the Christmas tree of eternal life and wonder!

The central point in this discussion is the fact that your faith grows in proportion to your knowledge of the Scriptures. Dwight L. Moody once said, "I prayed for faith and thought that some day faith would come down and strike me like lightning. But faith did not seem to come. One day I read in the tenth chapter of *Romans,* 'Now faith cometh by hearing, and hearing by the Word of God.' I had closed my Bible and prayed for faith. I now opened my Bible and began to study, and faith has been growing ever since."[11]

Right here is the key to the conquest of fear. I want to give you a little homework. Turn to *Luke* 12:4–34, a passage rich in discussion of the subjects of fear, worry, and anxiety. Note the vivid imagery: sparrows, ravens, hair, barns, lilies, purses, flocks, etc. Follow the flow of Christ's thought—its progression and logic. He is explaining the key to two of life's greatest mysteries—namely, how to overcome fear and how to have faith. I encourage you to pursue this exercise diligently and imaginatively, and if you do I doubt you will ever forget it. In your next frightening situation you will be able to reason, for example, "I may get fired, but I'll never be without life's necessities, for the Father promised that my food, drink, and clothing are guaranteed to me." The performance of this homework could be for you the start of an entirely new method of Bible study—the Imagination Method.

NOTES

1. *Webster's New Collegiate Dictionary* (Springfield, Mass.: G. C. Merriam, 1979), p. 566
2. *Psalm* 91:11

3. *Psalm* 46:11 (Living Bible)

4. *Hebrews* 11:1

5. *Hebrews* 11:27 (King James Version)

6. *Zephaniah* 3:15–17

7. *Luke* 8:22

8. *Hebrews* 11:17–19

9. *Genesis* 22:5

10. Corrie Ten Boom, *Tramp for the Lord* (Old Tappan, N.J.: Fleming H. Revell, 1974), p. 40

11. Henry H. Halley, *Pocket Bible Handbook* (Chicago: Henry H. Halley, 1954), p. 5

17

Why Faith Can Banish Fear

Let us go exploring! I wish to lead you into, perhaps, some new territory in search of the foundations of faith. New, because I am talking about something other than Christian doctrine. I am exploring how doctrine impacts upon you personally. Let me paint the contrast for you in human relationships. Suppose your father were a famous politician—brilliant, personable, skilled. Those adjectives would be an apt description of the man—what we know about him and the way he behaves; if you will, his attributes. On the other hand I would wish to explore what it is like to be his child. Is it good? Are your needs met? Do you feel loved? Are these experiences consistent? Are they predictable? Similarly I want to explore what it is like to be a Christian. In this chapter I am talking not about God but about you. In the list of beliefs that follow, we will scarcely even mention the name of God, although the actions and attitudes of God are the basis of these beliefs. These, I believe, are the main truths that, when believed, assure the conquest of fear in our lives.

YOU ARE LOVED.

This, I believe, is the belief most necessary to the conquest of your fear.

The constitution of human nature makes the feeling of love absolutely essential to one's security. All of us need love, for it fills a vacuum in our lives. An individual could be almost complete within himself were it not for the requirement for love. Infants can die for the lack of it. Those who did not have love in childhood exhibit a life-long hunger for it and for someone to be cast in the image of a father or a mother. Lovelessness is the seed of insecurity, and the person who does not feel loved requires the acceptance and approval of almost everyone he meets in order to feel safe.

On the other hand the feeling that one is loved produces strength in a life. It has been said that an infant's first sense of accomplishment is his ability to attract his mother's love. Every secure individual, whether child or adult, has under his feet the firm ground of knowing that he is loved. The Bible affirms that "perfect love drives out fear."[1]

In constructing your faith system, you should begin with the belief that you are the object of love. Mainly God loves you. The doctrine of the Bible begins with the concept that God loves all human beings. You do not have to strive to attract love for you are already loved. This teaching may sound trite to Christian people, and yet many Christians do not actually feel love. At least they do not live as if they were well loved. What is the problem? The problem is a matter of faith: they do not *believe* that they are loved. Their knowledge of God's love for them has not sunk deep into their hearts. Their emotions belie their unbelief. We all need to work constantly on our belief in God's love for us. *Sense* his love often and *imagine* it regularly in your life. God will not let you suffer harm, for he loves you. Armed with the knowledge that you are loved, you have nothing to fear.

LIFE IS GOOD.

As simple a statement as this is, many people appear not to believe it. Pessimism prevails in many lives. There is talk about the "human predicament," as though life were a quandary; about "no exit," as though people lived in a prison. Great and reputable authors and leaders announce their own disillusionment.

The Christian experience is diametrically opposed to such pessimism. A Christian's joy may even be so profound as to cast doubt upon the veracity of those who say they see life otherwise. Recently I stepped off an elevator in a building in New York City and walked down a hallway toward a private art gallery. When I opened the door to enter, I casually spoke to the doorman saying, "Hello."

Immediately he said, "Here's a man who says hello. Any man who says hello must be happy."

I just said, "Well, I've got a reason to be happy," and walked on in.

All of us have a reason to be happy, because life *is* good. This is our faith. We believe life to be good, and therefore we expect it to be. It always has been; it always will be. That is the way God makes it. Indeed, we would be surprised if life were not good to us. Few things have ever happened to me that were really "bad." Some things seemed bad at the time, but as I look back on them, I thought they were bad not because of what I was experiencing at the time, but because of what I feared would follow. The negative results which I feared rarely materialized. My fear created the badness. Having now lived so many years and having seen the pattern repeat itself so many times, I have finally become convinced that life is always going to be good. While I do not yet qualify for senior citizen status, I have finally learned to say with the Psalmist, "I was young and now am old, yet I have never seen the righteous forsaken or their children begging bread."[2] Yes, life is good—always will be—so you have nothing to fear.

LIFE IS GETTING BETTER.

So many people speak of life as a decline. We talk of the "declining years." The sands in the hourglass are running down, the body is fading, the hairline receding, the family departing—

Faith sees it otherwise. Life is not running down; it is running up! It is growing, improving, beautifying, ascending! The ultimate basis of our faith in the improving life is our belief in heaven. The emotional significance of heaven is the belief that the best is yet to come. Therefore we may graph an upward scale of life, from here to there. The future belongs to the Christian. The poet expressed the Christian philosophy when he wrote[3]:

Grow old along with me!
The best is yet to be,
The last of life, for which the first was made:
Our times are in His hand

Who saith "A whole I planned,
Youth shows but half; trust God: see all, nor be afraid!"

The belief that life tends upward holds extremely practical advantages for us. For example, young adulthood for many people is a very trying time of life, or as Margaret Mead called it, "a period of storm and stress." A Christian youth can more easily tolerate this turbulence because he knows that life will not always be like this. Personally I was in college during that stormy period of life, being barely seventeen years of age when I started, and I can well remember my poignant feelings of despair in that institution. I had not learned to cope with fear. I felt lonely, inadequate, and insecure, and would return to my rented room frequently to throw myself across my bed in despair. The secret of my victory over that despair—I remember it as yesterday—was my basic belief that things would improve. I might have given up completely in those days had not the simple phrase, "Things will get better," kept coming into my mind again and again. Where did I acquire that belief? It was the instinctive conclusion of my Christian beliefs. For me those days of despair were short-lived and soon gone. Truly life has been upward ever since. The distress that you now feel, the depression, the unhappiness, the loneliness will improve one of these days, provided that you do not lose faith in God. Life is getting better, so you have nothing to fear about the future.

GOD'S WILL IS THE BEST THING THAT COULD HAPPEN TO YOU OR THOSE AROUND YOU.

This is the belief that God is truly guiding your life and guiding it well. It is clear Biblical doctrine. Take for example these verses: "Do not conform any longer to the pattern of this world, but be transformed by the renewing of your mind. Then you will be able to test and approve what God's will is—his good, pleasing, and perfect will."[4] God's will is "good" for you. For that matter, it is good in the superlative—it is the best.

The concept of God's will has two aspects. First God's will is a plan of action that one consciously chooses to follow simply because one believes it to be what God wants. It is based upon the belief that God has an individual plan for your life which he will reveal to you if you seek it. If you follow his plan, it will be the best thing that could happen to you or to your loved ones and friends. The pursuit of a life that consciously seeks to know and follow God's will at every turn is a way of life that not many people choose. It represents the zenith of commitment to God. Many people shrink from this kind of life because they fear it. To be sure, it does take a tremendous faith to live like this, and herein lies the secret, the conquest of fear by faith.

There is another aspect of God's will which is also important —the acceptance, even the welcoming, of events that are beyond our control. The second highest act of commitment to God, second only to the active pursuit of God's will as mentioned above, is the passive acceptance of God's will in the events beyond your control. It is not always easy to say, "The will of the Lord be done," but it is necessary. It means quietly accepting the seemingly bad circumstances along with the good. Both bad and good weather are the will of God, both hirings and firings, both pressure and relaxation. The doctrine that supports this interpretation of the will of God is the belief that God is directing our total lives. As Browning said before, "Our times are in His hand." By way of limitation, this does not mean God causes everything that happens to us. He does not cause the evil that assails us. But God hems it in, limits it, curtails it, and often overrides it for our good.

Someone may object, "I certainly have not found that to be true. I have been observing for a long time, and I have not detected any plan of goodness or beneficence guiding my circumstances."

Perhaps you have failed to perform the experiment correctly. You have omitted the main ingredient: faith. The instructions for the experiment read like this: "Have faith in God and then observe that circumstances around you will be good and beneficial to you."

Someone may say, "Isn't that begging the question? It is like saying, 'Believe that God is guiding your circumstances, and then you can believe that God is guiding your circumstances.' "

No, I do not mean it like that. I mean that the condition is to "have faith in God." By "have faith in God," I mean genuinely having faith in him—totally dedicating yourself to him and his purposes. You see, you can have faith in God long before you even form any opinion concerning the effect of God upon the circumstances of your daily life. My point, though, is that after you have decided to exercise real faith in God, then you can look around and see—it may even surprise you—that all things have been working out for your good. Of course you must have faith first; that is the only way it works.

So, by trusting that God's will is the best thing that could happen to you or to those around you, you will have nothing to fear.

ALL YOUR NEEDS WILL CONTINUALLY BE MET.

This is such a common belief that I need say little about it. The Bible says it all: "My God will meet all your needs according to his glorious riches in Christ Jesus."[5] Yet when we are threatened, we forget it so easily. This gives us that much more reason to exercise faith in times of fear. Let faith be your memory aid to remind you of this promise. We all use mnemonics or memory aids to remind us of important things like, for example, tying a string around our finger. Let faith be your mnemonic. Imagine that you are wearing a signet ring on which are enscribed the words, "My needs will all be filled." Faith is that ring. Whenever you get into trouble, look at your imaginary ring and recollect this promise. Then you will have nothing to fear.

YOU CAN SURVIVE ANY TEST THAT COMES TO YOU.

One of the most assuring promises of all is this: "No temptation has seized you except what is common to man. And God is faithful; he will not let you be tempted beyond what you can bear. But when you are tempted, he will also provide a way out so you can stand up under it."[6]

One of the greatest and most common fears anyone ever faces is the fear of a breakdown. We fear that someday we will encounter some event so trying as to totally overwhelm our system. We say, "I see it happen to people everyday: nervous breakdowns, heart attacks during crises, stress-related illnesses, and so forth." We hear of tragedies and suspect that we could not tolerate such tragedies in our lives. We sometimes sense ourselves right on the brink of breakdown.

Nevertheless the promise is that nothing will happen to us that will exceed our breaking point. Now this is not to say we will be exempt from certain tragedies; it only affirms that no tragedy will totally defeat us. You must not say, "I could never tolerate this, that, or the other." You do not know what you could or could not tolerate. As a matter of fact, most of us live far below our tolerance zone. Go on a confidence course some weekend and you will see what I mean.

Yes, some people do experience breakdowns, and do you know why? Fear! For example, one says, "I'm *afraid* I'm going to have a nervous breakdown," and then has one. You see, the breakdown was self-induced by fear. This happens often.

I was living near the New York City harbor when one night a large ship plowed into the side of an oil tanker. Both vessels immediately caught fire, and crew members scrambled for their lives. The noise in the harbor awakened us, and we dashed to the roof of our highrise apartment building to view the flaming inferno below. For the captain of the ship at fault, this had been his very first cruise in the position of command. It seemed not to have been his fault, for the steering control broke at the time of the accident. However, he was guilty of inadvertently shouting the command, "Full steam ahead," when he discovered the problem. Most of the crew members on both ships survived the wreck but not that captain. No, he was not killed! He died on board his ship of a heart attack, and his crew carried his body to safety. What killed him? Probably nothing but fear! The fear that guilt produces, self-recrimination, self-reproach caused heart failure. Had he practiced faith thinking rather than fear thinking, he might still be alive today. Fear can do strange things to a person.

Defeat your fear by faith. Believe you will be the victor in all circumstances, and you will be. Choose faith and not fear. God's promises are triggered only by faith, but if you choose fear instead of faith, then God cannot deliver you from your self-induced defeats. And yet if you trust that you can survive any test life sends, then you have nothing to fear.

YOU HAVE NOTHING TO FEAR.

This belief, which I have already appended to the end of each of the six preceding beliefs, is now brought to the forefront. Certainly it is a cardinal point of Christian doctrine, and it needs to be singled out and spotlighted. I suppose this is not the kind of doctrine you will find included in a book on systematic theology, but maybe it should be. People need to have it taught to them as a valid point of doctrine so they can fall back upon it when times are frightening. We are taught that there is life after death, and we fall back upon that for comfort and strength when we lose our loved ones. Why do we not proclaim a doctrine that says God will deliver us from anything that produces fear, in order that we may fall back upon that doctrine, too, in times of fright and intimidation?

The abundance of biblical material provided so far supports the fact that this is biblical doctrine. Christ's challenge to the disciples in the boat—"You of little faith, why are you so afraid?" —implied this doctrine. If they did not have to fear death by drowning, then they had nothing to fear. The threat to Paul in his Mediterranean storm was much greater than theirs on the Galilean Sea, and yet even in that menace, Paul was comforted with the words, "Do not be afraid, Paul."[7] So certain is the assurance of this doctrine that we can, I believe, paraphrase Paul's words like this: "For I am convinced that neither death nor life, neither angels nor demons, neither the present nor the future, nor any powers, neither height nor depth, nor anything else in all creation, will be able to threaten us because of the love of God that is in Christ Jesus our Lord."[8]

This last belief, "You have nothing to fear," summarizes the others. If you make these seven statements the beliefs of your life and commit them to memory, you can be delivered from the fear of any danger that will ever confront you:

1. You are loved.
2. Life is good.
3. Life is getting better.
4. God's will is the best thing that could happen to you or to those around you.
5. All your needs will continually be met.
6. You can survive any test that comes to you.
7. You have nothing to fear.

NOTES

1. *1 John* 4:18
2. *Psalm* 37:25
3. Robert Browning's "Rabbi Ben Ezra"
4. *Romans* 12:2
5. *Philippians* 4:19
6. *1 Corinthians* 10:13
7. *Acts* 27:24
8. *Romans* 8:38, 39

18

"The Source of My Courage Was Faith"

Lest you think all this to be visionary and impractical, I offer two lively examples to illustrate that faith does work. Joshua and David came onto the scene with a dynamic faith and departed it many years later with the same powerful asset. We shall consider Joshua first.

Joshua was an aide to Moses throughout the wilderness wandering of the exodus and was Moses' successor to lead the Israelite refugees into the Promised Land. Conveniently the report of his life was broken into two parts—youth and old age—with no information in between the two. This enables us to lay the two parts side by side and to contrast them directly.

We see Joshua first as a young warrior in the first month of the exodus from Egypt.[1] Moses commanded him to choose some men to go out to fight the Amalekites. Joshua did so and decisively won the battle. Why do you suppose Joshua was the one selected? It was not because of his fighting ability, for this was the very first battle in Hebrew history and Joshua would not have had any experience on which he could have been evaluated. Perhaps it was an ability to lead men, which Joshua might have demonstrated in the days prior to departing Egypt. Whether it had been observed in advance or not, Joshua's ability to lead and to fight was well confirmed by the results of this battle. It was phenomenal for him to be able to convert within the space of one month an undisciplined crowd of slaves into a mighty army. From what happened later, however, we have reason to believe it was something other than innate ability and skill that first brought Joshua to Moses' attention. Let us hold that question in abeyance a while longer.

The next major event occurred a few months later at Kadesh

Barnea, where Moses assembled a small task force to reconnoiter the Canaanite borderland.² He hand-picked twelve men for the force, each representing one of the tribes. It was Joshua who was picked to represent the tribe of Ephraim. The mission of the spies was to enter Canaan, gather information, pick up some fruit from the land, and return within forty days.

The task force accomplished its mission and returned at the end of forty days with a single cluster of grapes so large it had to be carried on a pole between two men. The whole camp gathered in curiosity to hear the report and sample the grapes. The initial report was unanimous: Canaan was a fantastic place. The land fulfilled their fondest expectations. It did flow with milk and honey. However, the inhabitants were very powerful. It was not an unpopulated territory but was occupied by five different tribes: the Amalekites, the Hittites, the Jebusites, the Amorites, and the Canaanites. Their cities were large and well-fortified. The task force even saw some giants. As they talked on, the progress of the report was suddenly interrupted by one of the spies, Caleb, who sensed the negative drift of the words and quickly interjected: "We should go up and take possession of the land, for we can certainly do it."

Quickly the rest of the spies took to the defense and passionately objected: "We can't attack these people; they are stronger than we are. The land devours the occupants. All the people we saw there are of great size. We seemed like grasshoppers in our own eyes, and we looked the same to them."

The camp went into a tizzy of fear. All night long they wept and cried out, and an insurrection against Moses began brewing. Caleb, supported by Joshua, Moses, and Aaron, defended his optimism: "If the Lord is pleased with us, he will lead us into that land, a land flowing with milk and honey, and will give it to us. Only do not rebel against the Lord. And do not be afraid of the people of the land because we will devour them. Their protection is gone, but the Lord is with us. Do not be afraid of them."

The furor persisted, and the whole camp talked of stoning the four. Suddenly in the midst of the hubbub, the glory of the Lord appeared over the tabernacle, greatly sobering the people. When Moses went into the tabernacle to commune with the Lord, God met him with an angry offer to destroy the Israelites and create a people of God from the seed of Moses. The urgent, unselfish intercession of Moses that followed is one of the paramount examples of prayer anywhere in the Bible. God honored that intercession and spared the people, but he fulfilled his intent by destroying the spies, excepting only Caleb and Joshua from among them. Then in a presumptuous show of false repentance, the Israelites mustered their forces anyway and charged up into the hills to attack the Canaanites. In no sense was this an act of faith, and to their utter humiliation they were mercilessly attacked and soundly defeated. Their dreads were exactly fulfilled, for the land did "devour" them.

From this we gain a new insight into the reason for Moses' favoritism toward Joshua. It was not his skills, knowledge, or competencies; but it was his attitude, namely his faith, that commended him to Moses. I point this out for the encouragement of each reader. You may not be blessed with exceptional skills, either innate or learned. The image you project may not commend you to observers as an outstanding personality. For this reason you may despair of attaining greatness or for that matter even nominal success. Yet you need not be pessimistic. The example of Joshua suggests the possibility of achieving success apart from your limited skills or capacity but rather on the basis of the amount of faith you have. When General William Booth, founder of the Salvation Army, was asked the secret of his success, he replied, "God has had all there is of me. There have been many others who had greater plans, greater opportunities than I, but from the day I had a vision of what God could do, I made up my mind God would have all there was of William Booth." We have reason to believe Joshua was not originally a person of great gift and promise, for he was described at first only as Moses' "aide" or minister, which does not seem a very impressive description for a brilliant young man. Moses selected Joshua as his protégé because he saw in Joshua the trait which he himself most greatly valued: faith in God. Joshua was a man after his own heart. Faith can be your road to greatness too.

It was Joshua's faith that accounted for his superb courage. In his youth he never showed the least sign of fear. His bravery stood in stark contrast to the cowardice of those around him. The Israelites were a timid lot, afraid of the fiery mountain, afraid of captivity, afraid of foreign armies, afraid of chariots and horses and walled cities and giants. Joshua, on the other hand, dared to take risks, to speak against the majority, to defy foe and friend alike, to brave the odds, all because he believed strongly in the Lord God.

Joshua's defiance of giants epitomizes his fearlessness. With Caleb he held them in utter contempt, refusing even to address them as a significant problem in the minority report to the people. In the historical era in which they lived there existed a super-large race of men straight out of the past. Their dimensions were colossal—spearheads weighing in the pounds, spear shafts like weavers' beams, gigantic swords. King Oz of Bashan was one such pompous giant, later slain by Joshua, whose chief claim to fame was a bed thirteen feet long by six feet wide. Talk about a kingsize bed! As the last survivors of an era when physical might guaranteed success, these ancient occupants of Palestine were on the wane. They were more brawn than brain and were out of place in a generation when mental acumen was on the rise. Poor fellows! For their survival it would have been better to have retired them to the camel ranches rather than to have continued to thrust them forward on the battlefields. Leaders with more intelligence, though, were continuing to coax them forward in battle for their shock value to the enemy. Armies continued to be intimidated by them, but the newly emerging tacticians had begun to outsmart the slow-witted creatures and to turn their gigantic size into liabilities. While others were falling for the giants' bluffs, Joshua's faith, cushioning his fears, enabled him to disregard their threat totally. To him "the bigger they are, the harder they fall."

There are giants in your life too. They appear formidable, but in reality they are remnants of a waning generation. Your faith in God is the great equalizer to any problem you may ever confront. Faith is your compensator, your combat multiplier. By it you can move mountains. Elevate your faith to the level of the problems that confront you. Always remember, "If God is for us, who can be against us?"[3]

Next we see Joshua in the latter days of his life, as an elder statesman. Following the abortive invasion of Canaan at Kadesh-Barnea described earlier, an almost unbroken silence fell upon the young nation. When the story takes up again, all the adults who had left Egypt had died except Joshua, Caleb, and Moses. Prior to the final successful invasion of the land, Moses too had passed away; but Joshua still remained, with the same sterling character we saw four decades earlier. Added to his quality of faith is faith's close parallel and, indeed, spinoff: faithfulness. Time had validated Moses' selection of his protégé so that at the last Moses had felt free to choose him as his own successor. The elder Joshua, along with Caleb, falls heir to the honor and dignity that goes along with seniority, and yet it is not his age alone that distinguishes him. It is his faith. He is still the man of deep faith from forty years before. You can see it in his decisions, in his optimism, in his prayer life. He sets the pace for this new generation in the matter of confidence in a benign God.

Joshua's confidence does not reside in his seniority, nor for that matter in himself at all. His is not self-confidence, self-faith. Today many people have such a vague idea of what faith is. Whenever I ask people, "What should we have faith in?", frequently the reply comes back, "We should first have faith in ourselves." Not so! Godly faith is for those who cannot have faith in themselves. They know too well the depravity of their nature, the entrenchment of evil in their dispositions, the strength of temptation, and the weakness of their will. No, those who exercise true faith in God are those who hold their own persons in distrust and who have learned that to the degree they trust in anything else, to that degree they distrust God. Joshua held no faith in himself. Read carefully the encouragements spoken to him, first by Moses and then after Moses' departure by God himself. You perceive the image of a man distrustful of his own ability, prone to fearfulness, reluctant to lead, and repeatedly in need of assurance of the divine presence.

"But your assistant, Joshua the son of Nun, will enter it. Encourage him, because he will lead Israel to inherit it."[4]

"But commission Joshua, and encourage and strengthen him, for he will lead this people across and will cause them to inherit the land that you will see."[5]

"Be strong and courageous, for you must go with this people into the land that the Lord swore to their forefathers to give them . . . The Lord himself goes before you and will be with you; he will never leave you nor forsake you. Do not be afraid; do not be discouraged . . . Be strong and courageous."[6]

"Be strong and courageous . . . Be strong and very courageous . . . Be strong and courageous. Do not be terrified; do not be discouraged, for the Lord your God will be with you wherever you go."[7]

"The Lord said to Joshua, 'Do not be afraid of them . . .' "[8]

Those do not sound like words spoken to a super-confident man. We may learn a lesson from this. Faith thinking does not mean you are never afraid. It only means you know how to conquer fear whenever it arises. Joshua is never known to have committed even one act at the instigation of fear. Indeed in the era of his youth we would never have known him to be afraid, for only in his senior years is there a hint of fearfulness. Always, whether in his youth or in his old age, he counteracted fear by faith and never permitted the bud of fear to blossom into action. Then why the need for the constant encouragement? The reason is that those words were the nourishment for his faith. They enabled him to remain in the right frame of thought, namely, faith thinking. They reminded him that life is good and getting better, that God's plan is best, that all his needs would be met, that he would be used, that he had nothing to fear. Joshua's secret of success was not to remain courageous all the time but to have faith all the time.

Like Joshua's, our own faith needs encouragement constantly, and we need to read the Bible regularly, attend church, associate with faith thinkers, and pray daily for its encouragement. Our faith needs stimulating in all stages of our life. The faith of

Joshua's youth was not adequate for his old age, and neither will ours be. Indeed yesterday's faith is not adequate for today. "Give us today our *daily* bread,"[9] taught the Savior. As we are to pray for daily bread, so are we to pray for daily faith.

Before we leave this great man, let us observe the outcome of his faith in God. First his enemies came to fear him.[10] "Then all the peoples on earth will see that you are called by the name of the Lord, and they will fear you."[11] The majority were wrong when they saw themselves as grasshoppers in the eyes of their enemies. That's fear thinking! When the truth was known, the enemy saw them as the true giants to be feared, not as grasshoppers to be despised. Just remember that he who does not have faith has fear! If they are not doing faith thinking, they are doing fear thinking.

Second Joshua's success was complete and his victory was total. Curiously it is recorded that the Israelites conquered all the way to Kadesh Barnea, the site from which the spies were sent out forty years before.[12] Can you imagine Joshua's thoughts when his army, sweeping in from the north, cleared away the last remnants of opposition between him and Kadesh. Perhaps he stood on a hill observing that ancient campsite and thought to himself, "Indeed faith is the victory that overcomes the world."[13]

Third Joshua lived to see the end of war. "Then the land had rest from war."[14] This symbolizes the inward peace that always comes to one who has faith. In faith thinking not all is strife, risk, and hardship. When you have faith, at the very moment you have it, you also experience a personal peace that transcends explanation.

Finally Joshua experienced the serenity that capstones a life well lived. At one hundred ten years of age, he gathered the tribes together and gave his swan song, ending with those immortal words, "But as for me and my household, we will serve the Lord."[15] To the very end Joshua was a man of faith. Sweet serenity is the precious fruit of faith. If you are searching for serenity and quietness in your life, faith is the answer.

NOTES

1. *Exodus* 17:8–13
2. *Numbers* 13, 14
3. *Romans* 8:31
4. *Deuteronomy* 1:38
5. *Deuteronomy* 3:28
6. *Deuteronomy* 31:7, 8, 23
7. *Joshua* 1:6, 7, 9
8. *Joshua* 11:6
9. *Matthew* 6:11
10. *Joshua* 9:3, 9–24
11. *Deuteronomy* 28:10
12. *Joshua* 10:40–43
13. *1 John* 5:4
14. *Joshua* 11:23
15. *Joshua* 24:15

19

"I Fear No Evil"

You will discover, curiously, that King David stands as the Old Testament's main example of both faith and fearlessness. The advantage his life affords us is that it illustrates faith both by words and deeds. Whereas Joshua was a man of few words, David was a man of many words. Seventy-three of the Psalms are ascribed in their titles to him, in addition to his extensive recorded dialogue. Therefore we are better able to discern the connection between David's remarkable courage and his simple faith in God. In this chapter we will observe both his words and his actions as we study first the 23rd Psalm and second the conquest of Goliath.

HE KNEW THE SHEPHERD

In the 23rd Psalm David boasted, "I will fear no evil." Those were fabulous words unless they could be proven in action. David did prove them. He was one of history's most courageous men. Though his mettle was tested many times, he never "lost his cool." He was often the voice of courage amidst panic. Often his was the only portrait of confidence in a gallery of faintheartedness. Whereas at times both friend and foe were frightened and terror-stricken, seldom was fear attributed to David. Even when he was a solitary fugitive, he remained a man of prowess and daring. Possessed with a tranquil mind, his private life was quiet and calm. Worry or anxiety were never traits of his, and his sleep was serene. He wrote:

> I lie down and sleep;
>   I wake again, because the Lord sustains me.

> I will not fear the tens of thousands
> > drawn up against me on every side.[1]

What was the secret of David's fearlessness? He answers that question unequivocally: "I will fear no evil, for you are with me." Let us look at the context of these words. They are from the "Shepherd Psalm," written perhaps in his youth while still a shepherd, in which David pictures God as a shepherd and himself a sheep. He begins speaking of God in the third person but changes in the middle to the second person. In other words he changes it into a prayer.

> Even though I walk
> > through the valley of the shadow of death,
> I will fear no evil,
> > for you are with me;
> your rod and your staff,
> > they comfort me.[2]

Clearly he attributes his fearlessness to his faith in the Lord God. By faith he senses the Lord walking with him, even when his life is threatened. His faith is no detached sensation; it affects his emotions. It makes him brave. It causes him to live as if, in reality, God were actually by his side. Faith, to David, was not just a mood reserved for contemplation. Being intensely a man of action, he applied his faith to his everyday life. He trusted God to the very ultimate, even to the threat of his own death.

David, while never mentioning the word "faith," uses the similar word "trust" often.

> For the king trusts in the Lord;
> > through the unfailing love of the Most High
> > he will not be shaken.[3]

> Vindicate me, O Lord,
> > for I have led a blameless life;
> I have trusted in the Lord
> > without wavering.[4]

By *trust* David includes the three elements of faith described earlier—fellowshipping, sensing, and imagining. David seems to be aware that by the activation of this faith he is enabled to remain fearless.

1. FELLOWSHIPPING. From his very earliest days, David fellowshipped with the person of the living God. He sustained a personal relationship with God:

> Search me, O God, and know my heart;
> > test me and know my anxious thoughts,
> See if there is any offensive way in me,
> > and lead me in the way everlasting.[5]

He felt God's love for him individually:

> Many are the woes of the wicked,
> > but the Lord's unfailing love
> > surrounds the man who trusts in him.[6]

> Let the morning bring me word of your unfailing love,
> > for I have put my trust in you.[7]

The only times David felt detached from this very intimate relationship with God was when he knew he was guilty of sin against God, as during the nine months of Bathsheba's pregnancy; and yet even then David trusted that confession and repentance would restore the relationship. The depth of misery David experienced when he was apart from God (as recorded in *Psalms* 32 and 51) exemplified how much David valued that personal relationship. David believed God loved him enough to forgive his sins or to overlook minor infractions of the code, such as illegally eating the shewbread from the altar during a time of hunger when he was fleeing from Saul.[8] David's heart was in the right place for which he was described as a man after God's own heart.[9]

David was able to maintain the fine balance between his private and his public faith that is so difficult to maintain. Some people appear to be more devout in public than they actually feel, but David's private spiritual life far outweighed his public displays. His outward religion was merely the tip of the iceberg, the outer expression of his inward faith. Although he lived a very sincere, contemplative life, he never despised organized religion. In fact it was he who has been credited with organizing the Hebrew religion in the first place. What Moses began, David completed; he established religion and gave it a home. But the actions David took in the establishment of religion truly grew out of his own personal love for God. He had a lifetime ambition to build God a great temple simply because he wanted God to have a building superior to his own lavish palace. Generally David's rich personal fellowship with God set a dynamic example of what genuine faith should be like.

2. SENSING. Ofttimes David sensed the presence of God beside him. "You are with me," he said. He was very careful usually not to presume upon God because he felt a very real awe of God. He often sensed the *numinous* in his presence. One such occasion occurred when he was moving the ark of the covenant into the city of Jerusalem for the first time.[10] For seventy years it had been in the possession of an Israelite in a small village, but David determined to bring it to his capitol. A crude procession was arranged with music, instruments, and dancers accompanying an ox-drawn cart carrying the ark. En route one of the men committed an act of disobedience against God by touching the sacred chest for which he was stricken dead. David first grew angry and then waxed fearful. He literally sensed there the awesome presence of the living God.

3. IMAGINING. Many instances illustrate the imaginative way David experienced his faith in God, not the least of which was his Shepherd Psalm. His mind poetically employed the most common objects around him as vehicles for his faith. In the pasture he imagined God to be a shepherd. While enjoying his own home, he contrived to build God an even nicer home. In the mountain stronghold, he called God a "Rock"; at home he called him his "Father."[11] Listen to the novel ways he used familiar experiences to compose his devotions:

The Lord is my light and my salvation—
whom shall I fear?
The Lord is the stronghold of my life—
of whom shall I be afraid?
When evil men advance against me
to devour my flesh,
when my enemies and my foes attack me,
they will stumble and fall.
Though an army besiege me,
my heart will not fear;
though war break out against me,
even then I will be confident.[12]

THE GIANT KILLER

Having observed how David described his faith in God, let us now observe how he lived it. David was both a sayer and a doer of the word. His psalms provide us with a commentary upon his life. As a sample of the whole of his life, we will focus only on his battle with Goliath.

General Foch of World War I fame once said, "Battles are won the day before." Clearly, too, David's battle with Goliath was won before by a shepherd boy slinging rocks at cactus plants. David practically acknowledged that in saying, "Your servant has been keeping his father's sheep. When a lion or a bear came and carried off a sheep from the flock, I went after it and rescued the sheep from its mouth. When it turned on me, I seized it by its hair, struck it, and killed it. Your servant has killed both the lion and the bear; this uncircumcised Philistine will be like one of them because he has defied the armies of the living God."[13]

I propose we reexamine the story of David and Goliath from the viewpoint of fear and faith. During a particular season of war with the Philistines, David's three oldest brothers were deployed with King Saul's army. David, the youngest in the family, apparently was too young to fight. He was not too young to shepherd his father's flock, though, and was doing so at the time. Having just studied the 23rd Psalm, you may find it intriguing to learn that David probably wrote this psalm during this time. It was a season of faith building for him.

One day David's father sent him to the army camp to deliver some supplies to his brothers. He was excited when he got there to see the army moving into its battle line across a valley from the enemy formation. Eagerly David ran to his brothers in their battle positions just in time to witness the booming challenge to the Israelites from the huge enemy warrior, Goliath. What he saw left David aghast, both the blasphemous challenge of the giant and the cowardly response of his countrymen. Every last Hebrew soldier broke and ran. Quickly David started asking questions, "Who is this uncircumcised Philistine that he should defy the armies of the living God?"

Here David's actions may have been suspect of youthful bravado—as well his brother charged him—except that the following events proved them sincere. What do you suppose was David's emotion at the time? Was it not anger? He, for one, was not scared. He was mad! He loved God, and it vexed him to hear God's name maligned. That is faith—the evidence of a personal world view so real to David that you would have thought the man had insulted his mother. You see David's faith just swallowing up his fears. It was as though he forgot to be frightened. The honor of his very dearest friend was at stake, and it would have been a disgrace for him to put his own safety ahead of justice. That seemed to be David's first reaction that morning.

The lesson is that faith puts you into the perspective of an entirely unique world view. You think differently from other people. David's perspective was fresh that day. He had just come from meditating in the field, from praying, perhaps from singing God's praise. He was much more in touch with the positive values of the church than he was with the negative thinking of the army camp. They caught David at a time of faith thinking, but then faith thinking was more his norm than fear thinking.

Well, David got the facts, and then he volunteered to champion God's cause. So they took this strange young, auburn-haired Jew to the king. King Saul patronized David with some fatherly dissuasion, but the young man persisted in offering to fight Goliath. Here he made the statements recorded at the beginning of our story: he had slain a lion and a bear. Then he capped off these words by saying, "The Lord who delivered me from the paw of the lion and the paw of the bear will deliver me from the hand of this Philistine."

Again the key to David's courage emerges—his faith. Indirectly he attributed his conquest of the lion and bear to the Lord. His past experiences with these creatures had proven to his complete satisfaction the mighty power of faith. Now he was ready to risk his faith in an even more dangerous encounter.

Have you ever seen a person of deep faith in action? Some of the risks they take will take your breath away. Real faith is not something reserved for the churchhouse or private chamber. It is equally at home in the schoolroom, the marketplace, at the stadium, the barracks, anywhere and everywhere that fearful circumstances arise. Look at David. He was very meditative, but he was anything but a recluse. Distinctly he was a man of action, but when he acted, he usually acted out of faith. Like David, a person of faith has a very rich inner life but an equally rich outer life.

Somehow King Saul felt persuaded by young David and proceeded to commission him to duel with the giant. As David took up the task, you see the wisdom with which he moved, a wisdom made possible by the absence of fear. You see it first in his declining of Saul's armor. Since Saul stood head and shoulders above the average man, his armor would have been ill-fitting to David. Besides, David had never trained in armor. You see his wisdom, second, in his tactics. By taking his shepherd's staff with him onto the battlefield, he disguised his true weapon and deceived Goliath. Seeing the staff but not the sling, the Philistine said, "Am I a dog that you come at me with *sticks?*" Too late he saw the sling, for his shield was still with his armor bearer.

As the two adversaries approached one another, first Goliath spoke and then David. Very clearly David announced his exact intentions: he would strike Goliath down and cut off his head. Mainly though he announced his absolute dependence upon God for the results: "I come against you in the name of the Lord Almighty, the God of the armies of Israel . . . This day the Lord will hand you over to me . . . The whole world will know that it is not by sword or spear that the Lord saves; for the battle is the Lord's, and he will give all of you into our hands."

Someone may be prone to say, "Well, that just goes to prove that David was naturally a brave man."

That person may be wrong. Was David a "naturally" brave man? We cannot say whether or not he was "naturally" brave because we have no record of what David was like before he had faith in God. We do know this, that David attributed his courage simply to faith in God, not to nature, for he explained:

> When I am afraid
> I will trust in you.
> In God, whose word I praise,
> in God I trust; I will not be afraid.
> What can mortal man do to me?[14]

Returning to David's speech to Goliath, I greatly admire his kind of faith, the kind that claims the results even before they happen. David did not do that often, and I would not advocate anyone trying it except under the most certain of conditions. What are such conditions? There are two: First, when the results are sure to bring more glory to God than to any human being. Second, when the results are clearly and unmistakenly promised in the Bible.

In the final analysis David's faith in God was rewarded, as it always will be. David slung his sling, and God guided the stone directly to its target. On the assurance of the Word of God, you can be confident that faith thinking will never fail you: "Everyone who trusts in him will never be put to shame."[15]

NOTES

1. *Psalm* 3:5, 6
2. *Psalm* 23:4
3. *Psalm* 21:7
4. *Psalm* 26:1
5. *Psalm* 139:23, 24
6. *Psalm* 32:10
7. *Psalm* 143:8

8. *1 Samuel* 21:6
9. *1 Samuel* 13:14
10. *2 Samuel* 6
11. *Psalms* 18:31; 89:26
12. *Psalm* 27:1–3
13. *1 Samuel* 17
14. *Psalm* 56:3
15. *Romans* 10:11

PART IV

The Rewards of a Fear-Free Life

20

If There Were a Perfectly Fearless Person

Let us try to imagine what a perfectly fearless person would be like. I say "imagine" because I doubt anyone in our immediate acquaintance meets that description. Certainly it is not I. According to our theory, we must immediately say that such a person would have perfect faith. In the seesaw effect, for fear to be at the very bottom, faith would have to be at the very top. This person would sense God's presence continually, fellowship with God regularly, and imagine eternal truths wholly. He or she would believe absolutely in God's love and God's control over the total life of the believer. Circumstances that seemed harmful would not be judged hastily pending the unfolding of their results. Such a one would believe that ultimately everything would work out for his or her good. This person would fear no evil, not even death, and would believe resolutely in life after death.

If we ever met anyone without fear, this person would be very courageous and lionhearted. Lacking entirely the element of fear, this one would always endeavor to achieve whatever he or she felt to be right or necessary, no matter what the cost. Without even trying, such a one would appear to be a model of daring and heroism. This person's total life would be a great adventure.

The fearless person would also seem very strong. Not being afraid of what anyone says or thinks, this individual would think, decide, and act for himself or herself. Immune to intimidation, such a one could not be beaten, brought to the knees, or put to shame.

The unfearing person would also seem very outspoken because such a one would not be afraid to speak his or her mind. If we judge objectively, we must conclude that this person would always stand by the truth, because failing to do so, he or she would be subject to guilt. Guiltiness is one of the forms of fear—the fear of retribution. By always taking a stand for the truth, such a person would have no fear of the criticism of others.

Being rid of fear, such an individual would appear perfectly · calm, poised, peaceful, and serene. In spite of opposition or persecution, this person would never seem agitated, confused, or hurried.

Significantly the fearless one would feel a strong identification with other people. This person would never be stand-offish from others, because of the sympathy and instinctive feeling this one would have for the feelings of others. Such a person would sense deeply the fears of others. Though he or she may never yield to fear, this person would be tempted by it and therefore would be well acquainted with all of fear's guises and symptoms. This one would feel deep pity for the victims of fear.

The unfearing person would be one of deep love. Being a person of perfect faith as well as of perfect fearlessness, this one would reflect God's characteristic of love in his own life. Not fearing things or people, this one would be free to love others.

Finally the person with perfect fearlessness would be, for all appearances, a very joyful and happy individual. His or her sense of well-being would never be destroyed by events or circumstances. This one would seem to have the secret of the "good life." He or she would enjoy life at all times.

So these then are the main clues to the identification of the fearless person. If we ever decided to search for the person without fear, these would be the characteristics we would be looking for. That seems like an impossible blend, does it not? We have all known people with certain of these qualities in their lives in various mixes, but I doubt that we have ever known anyone with all of them. Some people are very daring, but they live anything but serene lives. Some are happy but appear weak. Some are outspoken but do not love people. In this book I have strongly advocated the possibility of living a fearless life, and you might say that the above is a description of the kind of life you could live if you could attain perfect fearlessness. It is a standard to strive for. And yet we always come back to the old adage, "No one is perfect."

And yet there *is* one person who can meet the description of the fearless person. Beyond a shadow of a doubt, Jesus of Nazareth lived a life that met all the qualifications of a perfectly fearless person.

Although he did not need faith personally—for he was truly God—Jesus did evidence the essential elements of faith: he sensed the presence of his Father continually, fellowshipped with him regularly, and imagined eternal truths wholly.

Jesus was very courageous and lionhearted. For example, he deliberately chose to return to Jerusalem at the height of his ministry (to the astonishment of his disciples), even though he knew he would be killed there.[1] Isaiah foretold his astonishing bravery in these words:

> He was oppressed and afflicted,
>> yet he did not open his mouth;
> he was led like a lamb to the slaughter,
>> and as a sheep before her shearers is silent,
>> so he did not open his mouth.[2]

Jesus also gave the appearance of great strength to everyone he met, even his enemies. When an angry crowd in Nazareth tried to force him over a cliff, "he walked right through the crowd and went on his way."[3] When temple guards were sent to arrest him, they were so surprised at his personal power that they dared not lay a hand on him. When finally an entire detachment of soldiers got the nerve to arrest him in the Garden of Gethsemane, they fell backward to the ground when they first saw him. I think that must have been a comic scene—armed soldiers picking themselves up from the ground and brushing themselves off before they realized that Jesus, this time, was permitting himself to be arrested.

Jesus was also very outspoken. The Pharisees were incredulous that his denunciations of them should be so bold and blatant, and his disciples asked him solicitously, "Do you know that the Pharisees were offended when they heard this?"[4] Yes, he knew, but so what? It was the truth!

Jesus always exhibited calmness, poise, peace, and serenity.

The most fitting illustration of this was the experience that provides the model for this book: the sea storm. It is a downright wonder that Jesus could sleep through the storm and have to be awakened to learn about it! His was a soul perfectly at peace with itself.

Jesus felt a strong identification with the fearful, the sick, and the confused. He showed profound concern, especially for frightened women.

He was also a person filled with love. The apostle John referred to himself as "the disciple whom Jesus loved."[5] And when Jesus wept at the tomb of Lazarus, the Jews exclaimed, "See how he loved him!"[6]

Finally, Jesus fit the condition of being a happy, joyful individual. He was described as being full of joy, and he expressed his assurance that the joy he experienced would be reproduced within his followers. He disdained his enemies' shameful treatment of himself because of the joy that was set before him. Jesus bore all the markings of a perfectly fearless person.[7]

The question arises, "What does the fearlessness of Christ have to do with me?"

Why, it has everything to do with you, for his fearlessness is transferable to you! By faith you may receive his very own boldness and courage with all their accompanying symptoms. His qualities of courage, strength, candor, serenity, love, and joy can be reproduced in your life. To be sure, the life of Jesus is the ideal model of the kind of life that results from the practice of conquest by faith.

In the New Testament, you can see how the courage of Christ was transferred to others. You can see the "before" and the "after." Before, his disciples were timid and fearful. After, they were as bold as lions. In the storm-tossed boat, all the disciples were caught stickily in the web of fear, and the only one among them with courage was their Master. His courage was unfathomable, as is evidenced by his peaceful slumber through it all. While they had great fear, he had no fear! It was at that time he revealed to them the secret of the conquest of fear in the simple statement, "You of little faith, why are you so afraid?" With faith they could conquer their fears.

The "after" for the disciples came following Jesus' resurrection and ascension. During the period of the sweeping evangelistic campaign in Jerusalem, the new valor of the disciples was remarkable. Despite opposition, danger, and threats, nothing could halt their bold witness. It was observed during that time: "When they saw the *courage* of Peter and John and realized that they were unschooled, ordinary men, they were astonished and they took note that these men had been with Jesus."[8]

Observe several things about this statement. For one, it was just the plain, simple courage of Peter and John that most impressed the witnesses. It was not their holiness, righteousness, saintliness, or enthusiasm. For another, the public had difficulty explaining the source of their courage. Their first hypothesis was that they were educated men—apparently, educated men appeared bolder than others in those days—but they ruled that out. Not until they learned that the disciples had accompanied Jesus did they reach a satisfactory explanation. This indicated that the public held the personal courage of Jesus in high esteem. Those who had been on the site with Jesus agreed with our claim that Jesus was the model of perfect fearlessness. Not only so, but the witnesses to the fiery ministry of Peter and John seemed to instinctively realize that the courage of Jesus had transferred to his followers. This transference might have been explained by the fact that Jesus taught his followers boldness and courage. That in itself would be significant! Or the disciples might merely have caught the contagious courage of Christ Jesus from having been with him so much, just as someone catches the enthusiasm of another from extensive association with that person.

A saying once went the rounds, "Christianity is caught, not taught." Such appeared to be the case with the disciples, for they caught the spirit of Jesus: his boldness and fearlessness. After all, the Lord had predicted they would do so. He said, "Peace I leave with you; *my peace* I give you."[9] "Peace" here is to be understood as the serenity and quietness that comes with the removal of fear, for Jesus goes on to say, "Do not let your hearts be troubled and do not be *afraid.*" So Jesus was saying he would infect them with his own fearlessness. His own peace would flow over to them. He would share his serenity with them. If you have your New Testament opened to *John* 14 from which I am quoting, you can observe the process by which the peace of Christ was transferred to the disciples. It was communicated via their faith. The chapter begins with the challenge, "Do not let your hearts be troubled. *Trust* in God; *trust* also in me."[10] Since a troubled heart was synonymous with fearfulness (as we noted in verse 27), Jesus was simply saying trust or faith in him is the cure for fear. Eureka! We are back to our theme. But I want to push the subject one step farther this time. The implication of this is that faith was the process by which the peace of Christ—this untroubled heart, fearlessness, and boldness—was transferred to the disciples. Can you see how it happens? The Jews saw it! "They took note that these men had been *with* Jesus," had been with him in fellowship, in sensing, and in imagination, to use our three elements of faith. So by their faith Christ was enabled to transfer his peace unto them.

It still works today. As you fellowship with Christ in simple faith, a change begins to take place in you. A little of Christ begins to rub off on you. Just as a husband and wife grow similar to one another over the years, a person grows to be more like Jesus over years of association with him. Thus the amazing serenity of Christ can become yours by means of your faith in him.

NOTES

1. *Mark* 10:32
2. *Isaiah* 53:7
3. *Luke* 4:30
4. *Matthew* 15:12
5. *John* 13:23; 19:26; 21:7, 20
6. *John* 11:36
7. *Luke* 10:21; *John* 15:11; *Hebrews* 12:2
8. *Acts* 4:13
9. *John* 14:27
10. *John* 14:1

21
The Key to an Exciting Life

Yes, a deep change can take place within a person when he or she practices faith thinking. It is a positive change producing highly desirable mental and emotional results. Arnold H. Lowe spoke to this possibility in the title of a book he wrote: *Beliefs Have Consequences.* Let us analyze these consequences in the next two chapters. The first consequence of faith thinking is an exciting life.

Have you ever ridden on a roller coaster? I rode one once—a very small one—many years ago. This past summer I also took my family out to an amusement park and rode on the next thing to a roller coaster, a log flume! (I am glad I was not photographed on the downward slope!) Whatever our opinion of roller coasters may be, nothing changes the fact that they continue in popularity year after year. Mark that carefully! On a recent television program several people were interviewed who frequented a gigantic roller coaster in Cincinnati. For some of them, riding the coaster was like an addiction. One man said he rides it every afternoon after work; he had ridden it one hundred and six times. The program reported there are even roller coaster riders' conventions.

What makes roller coasters so popular? One would not think they could be, considering the fright they provoke. And yet people keep coming back. A ride operator said he has seen people faint on the roller coaster and return to ride it again an hour later. Is this some form of psychotic mania? No, it is just plain, ordinary people like you and me who are out seeking a thrill. I must confess that I too enjoyed the flume ride—after it was over —and I think I would enjoy the large roller coaster too, if I could get up the nerve to ride it. You see, I, also, like a thrill now and then. Here is what we are basically doing when we ride a roller coaster: we are toying with our fears—playing with them—teasing them. We are pretending to fool ourselves. It is as though we tell our psyche, "Look out now because I am going to put you into a terribly dangerous situation." Yet in the back of our minds we know it really is not dangerous, for when we rise to a frightening height, we know there is a mass of sturdy steelwork beneath us. And when we suddenly zoom downward, we know we are not in a fatal freefall. And when we jerk around a curve at a soul-shocking G-rate, we know we have a powerful bar holding us in place. And when we almost despair of coming out of the experience alive, we inwardly remember that thousands of others have walked away safely at the end, however wobbly their legs might have been. The very value in a roller coaster is in the false fear it creates in us—pseudo-fear. This is what makes it thrilling!

Apply this principle to the rest of your life. Your faith is the part of you that knows in your fearful situations that everything will turn out all right. Allegorically, when we rise to life's dangerous heights, we know by faith that there is a mass of sturdy steelwork beneath us. When life suddenly zooms downward, we know by faith that we are not in a fatal freefall. When we jerk around curves of rapid change at soul-shocking G-rates, we know by faith that we have a powerful bar holding us in place. And when we almost despair of coming out of some peril in one piece, by faith we know we will walk away from it safely in the end. Our lives are made thrilling by the pseudo-fear we experience in the process. God has designed life to be marvelously exciting, and it is our faith that turns disasters into adventures. That's part of God's plan! But our faith is necessary to the success of God's plan, just as faith is necessary to the rider on the roller coaster. If one did not have faith, at least a certain kind of faith, a roller coaster ride would be a terrifying experience, to be avoided at all costs. Those who do experience it would be confined to mental hospitals in catatonic states of frozen fright. But by means of his faith book, the Bible, God leads us to the base of each of life's roller coasters before we get onto it. He points and says, "See, this steel latticework is strong enough to support a tower. These clamps grip the rails so that it is impossible for the cars to jump the track. This bar across your lap could not be lifted by a crow bar. And most importantly here is the end of the ride where your car will glide to a smooth and safe stop. Fear not!"

Look at the Bible and see some of the experiences where God permitted a frightening situation, while giving enough data to turn a fright into a thrill if the person would dare to exercise faith. Before they got into the boat, for example, Jesus had invited the disciples to accompany him, saying, "Let's go over to the other side of the lake."[1] It was as though he showed them the end of the roller coaster ride before they got on; they would reach "the other side" in all safety. If they had had faith, their boat ride would have been a thrill, not a fright. Or take Moses' suffering in the wilderness: "He regarded disgrace for the sake of Christ as of greater value than the treasures of Egypt, because he was looking ahead to his reward."[2] So the exodus became his adventure.

God makes life worth living by putting excitement, adventure, and a thrill into it. The faith thinker's life is not bland, unstimulating, and uninvigorating. Truthfully I have literally had bone-crushing experiences of which I have said, "I would gladly go through that again for Christ's sake." The end of each of my experiences with Christ so far has been good.

Faith's optimism is justified because it is connected to reality. It is the mighty God who creates reality and who tells us what it is. When the Bible takes us to the terminal point of one of life's many roller coasters and shows us the way that incident will turn out, it is merely showing us the ultimate reality. For example, when you are riding on a literal roller coaster, your fears are telling you, "You're going to die," but your faith is telling you, "No, you are perfectly safe." Which one is describing reality? Your faith, of course! Sometimes you may get the impression that faith thinking and fear thinking are just two optional choices that we have—both equally weighted, both equally right. Not so! They bear this major difference: Faith thinking is reality thinking; fear thinking is unreality thinking.

More thrills and adventures than ever before abound in our fast-paced modern world. Many people are unable to enjoy them, however, because of their fears. They are like squalling children on a merry-go-round, unable to enjoy the fun because of their fears. On the other hand even the menaces of life can be thrilling provided we have faith in God to believe that life is good, that we can survive any test that comes our way, and that we have nothing to fear.

NOTES

1. *Mark* 4:35
2. *Hebrews* 11:26

22
Peace and Joy

PEACE

The second consequence of faith thinking is the feeling of personal peace. Peace comes because of the peculiar characteristics of fear and peace. Fear always has a way of working against one's inward peace to undermine, dilute, erode, and eventually destroy it. Fear is an antonym for peace. The rise of anxiety and the decline of serenity in society today are not unrelated phenomena. They have a cause-and-effect relationship, for our fears are robbing us of tranquillity. Ultimately our fears are the explanation for the many books today on peace of mind and emotion. I am persuaded, on the other hand, that peace is an innate quality of every human being, inborn and resident within one from the very beginning. But our inborn peace is easily disturbed whenever fear enters our minds. We lose it because of fear. A growing child knows happiness and peace until something intervenes to frighten him. This fright may come early, as a result of neglect or abuse. Or it may come later as a result of disappointments, peer disapproval, maladjustment, failures—those common tests so characteristic of the teen years. A gifted few may be late developers so far as fear is concerned, leading placid lives right on into adulthood, but being all the more devastated by fear when it comes, simply because they so little expected it. It is fear that produces the discord and unrest within us.

Indeed, with all of us there always abides in the deepest caverns of our minds that additional fear of divine judgment for our sins. (Pascal agreed, saying "In His will is our peace.") When we are not at peace with God, a pervading fear disturbs our inner peace until that fear is removed by reconciliation with God. Even the explanation for our fear of dying lies in our fear of judgment after death.

In general we all have peace, but it is buried under layers of fears, whether childhood fears, teenage fears, adult fears, or our universal fear of judgment and retribution. So peace is not a commodity to be added to us but a possession to be uncovered. How is peace uncovered? Simply by the removal of fear! I have noted earlier that peace is the absence of fear. When your fears are conquered, your peace will return.

This is not a new idea. God's Word affirmed it long ago: "Do not be anxious about anything . . . And the peace of God, which transcends all understanding, will guard your hearts and minds in Christ Jesus."[1]

Since faith conquers fear, we may also say that peace is the result of faith. Again the Bible affirms, "You will keep in perfect peace him whose mind is steadfast, because he *trusts* in you."[2]

Faith produces a tranquil mind. Isaiah wrote, "In quietness and trust is your strength."[3] Individual tranquillity can have far-reaching results. Dr. Jampolsky writes, "When our mind is filled with upsetting thoughts, we see the world and those in it as upsetting to us. On the other hand, when our mind is peaceful, the world and the people in it appear to us as peaceful."[4] The lack of quiet minds accounts for the abundance of marital, familial, criminal, and international disturbances today.

Faith produces contentment. How can one account for so much discontent in this, the most affluent age in history? The answer—fear. Mental unrest produces the most exaggerated forms of social conflict, as *James* explains:

> What causes fights and quarrels among you? Don't they come from your desires *that battle within you?* You want something but don't get it. You kill and covet, but you cannot have what you want. You quarrel and fight. You do not have because you do not ask God.[5]

Many people are consumed with fears over material possessions. They want more, but they greatly fear losing what they have. There is a dominating fear of deprivation that is unique to those who are wealthy, as is evidenced by the number of suicides on Wall Street in the Depression. The faith thinker, however, is blessed with a contentment unknown to everyone else. The statement has been well made that only Christians really know how to appreciate material possessions. They may lose what they have, but so what? There is more where it came from. The Lord is their provider.

Keep your lives free from the love of money and be content with what you have, because God has said, "Never will I leave you; never will I forsake you." So we say with confidence, "The Lord is my helper; I will not be *afraid.*"[6]

Faith produces a profound peace of mind. The faith thinker is like an ocean whose surface may be stormy at times but whose depth is always motionless. The fear thinker, however, is like an ocean whose surface may appear placid but whose depth is always turbulent. The faith thinker may continue to know trials, tribulation, sorrow, and loss, but underneath are the Everlasting Arms.

Ripley's Believe It or Not records the story of a doctor in Paris in 1845 who prescribed to a depressed person a visit to Debureau, the famous clown, because, "If he can't make you laugh, there is no hope for you." The sad man replied, "I am Debureau." A year later Jean Gaspard Debureau died, for no other reason than "extreme melancholia."

On the contrary, we who work with people and their problems often encounter the person who has every reason for despair yet somehow continues living victoriously. Only three weeks ago I learned that one of my fellow church members had just undergone exploratory surgery, only to be diagnosed with inoperable cancer. She was still in the recovery room when I got to the hospital. I met her husband and young adult daughter in the waiting room and accompanied them to the cafeteria for coffee. Afterward, when I was returning to the surgical ward on the elevator with the daughter, she said to me, "Maybe it hasn't hit me yet, but I have a strong feeling of peace about the situation." A few days later I spent a little time alone with the lady in her hospital room. I found her very resigned to the diagnosis. With a smile on her face she said, "I may have only six more months to live, but God has given me peace."

This is a reaction that I find repeatedly among people of faith. Believers, of course, have tranquillity when things are going smoothly, but who does not? It is when the troubles come that the real nature of their peace shows up. Years ago at a country church I received the following letter from an elderly widow who had just broken her leg (recorded just as she wrote it):

I have experience the time when I felt as if I would love to go away and leave it all behind and find some place that known to God alone. I git weary and heartsick of this life and long to go where I cand find peace for my weary sold and rest for my tird bodie. I feel as if I diden even as mutch as have a friend but I have found that there is no greater remedry then to take the dear book the bible and just go some place and sit down and read and think. Just sit still and count the blessings that are with in reach of my ears and eyes. Thank of him who givieth the richest blessings that I enjoy even if I did thank a little while ago that myne was all sadness and sorrow and heartakes in this life. Then when I rise with a prayer of thanksgiving in my heart then I go back to my wort and thank not on the dark side of life but upon my meny blessings.

JOY

Joy, the third consequence of faith thinking, is at the zenith of the products of faith. Of all the valued qualities resulting from faith thinking, genuine happiness is the most treasured. Courage is self-satisfying, excitement invigorating, and serenity desirable, but all are bland if there is no joy. Without joy, the brave person is only a martyr, the excited person a sensationalist, and the tranquil one a bore, none of which cuts a popular figure with the public. Joy is the quality that advertises faith as something more than a mere remedy. Medicine is a remedy, but it is unpopular as a beverage. Joy, however, is the beverage of life, the elixir of existence.

Joy is the quality that adds meaning to an event. When one goes to the theater, the question that people ask is this: "How did you *enjoy* the play?" We *enjoy* a football game, a certain dish, a sermon, a friendship, etc., or else it is not very highly valued. Even so, joy is the spice that puts the pleasure into life.

To get the best perspective for appreciating how important the fruit of joy can be in a life, I suggest you reflect on how little joy there is in the world. There really is not much! Some of the world's greatest thinkers agree on this. According to the standards of many, Napoleon Bonaparte should have been a joy-filled man. Yet in his biography he is quoted as saying, "I am seldom happy," to which he added, "but then what man is?" The famous British philosopher, David Hume, wrote in his volume *On Miracles*, "We can scarcely dream of happiness." Perhaps Hume's writings influenced the writers of the Constitution to speak of "life, liberty, and the *pursuit* of happiness." You can pursue it; you might not apprehend it! C. S. Lewis entitled his autobiography *Surprised by Joy* and told how he vainly pursued joy before finally finding it in Christ. The considered opinion of many knowledgeable people is that joy is one of the rarest commodities of life. If you lack joy yourself, there may be some consolation in knowing that many people consider joy to be nonexistent in our world. To be sure, many feign joy effectively, and you may have looked around at many seemingly happy people and wondered why you are so different. Why, you are probably in the majority!

And yet, real joy abounds in the faith thinker! Joy, too, is the absence of fear. What did the herald angel say? "Do not be *afraid.* I bring you good news of great *joy* which shall be for all the people."[7] Faith thinkers are not pretending when they say they have joy. Christ promised it. The disciples experienced it. Paul's letter to the Philippians, although penned while he was in prison, uses the words "joy" and "joyful" thirteen times. Every faith thinker I have ever met testified to genuine joy in his or her life.

·Joy will be your instant and immediate experience if you will have faith in Christ Jesus. You will not have to wait. Neither will you need anything else. In faith thinking joy is not contingent upon possessions, situations, environment, or companions. You have everything you need to be happy right now.

In those days of combat in Vietnam my battalion was the vanguard of the forces that entered Cambodia across the border from Pleiku. I spent ten solid days with them criss-crossing the path of the infamous Ho Chi Minh trail secreted within that towering teakwood jungle. Unspeakable danger abounded everywhere. As was my custom, I flew from company to company conducting services. Being yet unfamiliar with the conquering power of faith, though experimenting with it, I recall part of the message I preached to the men: "I am happy in Cambodia. Don't get me wrong. I am not saying I'm happy *to be in* Cambodia. But I am happy here—because of Jesus."

NOTES

1. *Philippians* 4:6, 7
2. *Isaiah* 26:3
3. *Isaiah* 30:15
4. Gerald G. Jampolsky, *Love Is Letting Go of Fear* (Toronto: Bantam Books, 1981), p. 72
5. *James* 4:1, 2
6. *Hebrews* 13:5, 6
7. *Luke* 2:10

CHRISTIAN HERALD ASSOCIATION AND ITS MINISTRIES

CHRISTIAN HERALD ASSOCIATION, founded in 1878, publishes The Christian Herald Magazine, one of the leading interdenominational religious monthlies in America. Through its wide circulation, it brings inspiring articles and the latest news of religious developments to many families. From the magazine's pages came the initiative for CHRISTIAN HERALD CHILDREN and THE BOWERY MISSION, two individually supported not-for-profit corporations.

CHRISTIAN HERALD CHILDREN, established in 1894, is the name for a unique and dynamic ministry to disadvantaged children, offering hope and opportunities which would not otherwise be available for reasons of poverty and neglect. The goal is to develop each child's potential and to demonstrate Christian compassion and understanding to children in need.

Mont Lawn is a permanent camp located in Bushkill, Pennsylvania. It is the focal point of a ministry which provides a healthful "vacation with a purpose" to children who without it would be confined to the streets of the city. Up to 1000 children between the age of 7 and 11 come to Mont Lawn each year.

Christian Herald Children maintains year-round contact with children by means of a *City Youth Ministry.* Central to its philosophy is the belief that only through sustained relationships and demonstrated concern can individual lives be truly enriched. Special emphasis is on individual guidance, spiritual and family counseling and tutoring. This follow-up ministry to inner-city children culminates for many in financial assistance toward higher education and career counseling.

THE BOWERY MISSION, located at 227 Bowery, New York City, has since 1879 been reaching out to the lost men on the Bowery, offering them what could be their last chance to rebuild their lives. Every man is fed, clothed and ministered to. Countless numbers have entered the 90-day residential rehabilitation program at the Bowery Mission. A concentrated ministry of counseling, medical care, nutrition therapy, Bible study and Gospel services awakens a man to spiritual renewal within himself.

These ministries are supported solely by the voluntary contributions of individuals and by legacies and bequests. Contributions are tax deductible. Checks should be made out either to CHRISTIAN HERALD CHILDREN or to THE BOWERY MISSION.

**Administrative Office: 40 Overlook Drive, Chappaqua, New York 10514
Telephone: (914) 769-9000**